W9-BDV-749

# The Mills at Winooski Falls

Winooski and Burlington, Vermont

# The Mills at Winooski Falls

## Winooski and Burlington, Vermont

*Illustrated Essays and Oral Histories*

Editor
Laura Krawitt
Director, Héritage Winooski

Editorial Assistant
Jeremy Felt
Professor Emeritus of History
University of Vermont

## ONION RIVER PRESS

WINOOSKI, VERMONT

Published by Onion River Press
Champlain Mill, One Main Street, Winooski, Vermont 05404

*About the Publisher*
Onion River Press is an independent publisher dedicated to creating books by Vermont authors or about Vermont. The Press publishes fiction, non-fiction and poetry titles representing unique voices, otherwise unheard in works produced by large, profit-driven publishing houses. Located in a former textile mill on the bank of the Winooski River, Onion River Press — whose name comes from the Abenaki 'winooski' meaning wild onions, which were found growing on the banks of the river — strives to introduce works of outstanding literary merit. Through its support of independent bookstores and their efforts to be integral members of their communities, the Press helps to ensure that diversity of voice and freedom of expression continue to thrive in the bookselling world. The green hills and independent spirit of Vermont have inspired many writers over the years, and Onion River Press' mission is to bring the uncommon perspective, the native voices and the extraordinary talents of Vermont's writers to others.

To receive our complete catalog, please contact Onion River Press, c/o The Book Rack & Children's Pages, Champlain Mill, One Main Street, Winooski, Vermont 05404, call us at (802) 655-0231 or e-mail us at bookrack@together.net.

Copyright © 2000 Laura Krawitt

All rights reserved. This book, or parts thereof, may not be reproduced in any form without permission from the editor.

Library of Congress Cataloging-in-Publication Data

The mills at Winooski Falls: Winooski and Burlington, Vermont: illustrated essays and oral histories / Laura Krawitt, editor; Jeremy Felt, editorial assistant.
    p. cm.
  Includes bibliographical references.
  ISBN 0-9657144-4-6
   1. Wool industry--Vermont--Winooski--History. 2. Wool industry--Vermont--Burlington--History. 3. Winooski (Vt.)--History. 4. Burlington (Vt.)--History. I.Krawitt, Laura P.

HD9897 . W56 2000
338.4'767731'0974317--dc21

Book design by Anne Linton

Cover: Photograph of Rose Wheel, c. 1943, by James Detore, a photographer for the *Burlington Daily News* during the 1940s. Rose Wheel was a twister at the American Woolen Company in Winooski; her machine reduced the diameter of wool roving to a smaller size for spinning. (Courtesy of Special Collections, University of Vermont Libraries)

Printed in the United States of America

To the authors for their contribution to the
mill history of Winooski Falls and Vermont.

# TABLE OF CONTENTS

# Acknowledgments

"Many hands make light work," the saying goes, and many hands indeed lent their help with this publication. A native of Winooski, Robert Picher furnished essential details. He and other readers, Dana Lim vanderHeyden, Saint Michael's College; Ned Caron, Winooski Public Schools; and Renée Reiner and Lynn Johnson, at the Book Rack, provided helpful comments and constructive criticism. Patricia Brennan, University of Vermont, helped with transcriptions.

Many of the contributors and their relatives furnished illustrations from family or business collections. In addition, Sister Marion Chaloux provided items from Fanny Allen Hospital archives. Darcy Coates and Christine Fearon helped with the Robert Hull Fleming Museum's collection of Lewis Hine photographs. From the Vermont Historical Society, Paul Carnahan and Jaqueline Calder offered suggestions about illustrations that otherwise would have been missed and Martha Nye's help saved trips to Montpelier. At the University of Vermont's Special Collections Department, Jeffrey Marshall was instructive as well as helpful with the selection of photographs. Connell Gallagher, Sylvia Bugbee, Karen Campbell and others of the library staff were always patient and willing to assist. Winooski Historical Society members Rita Martel, Mary Ellen Fitzgerald and Jeannine Picher cheerfully opened their museum to help locate photographs.

A special thank you to my husband, Edward Krawitt, University of Vermont, for his patience, support and constructive reviews, and to my friend Margaret Ritchie, free-lance editor, for her advice.

Light work this has been, a delightful experience learning so much about a special place, but with a certain sadness that Raymond Roy is no longer with us.

Laura Krawitt
August 2000

# Prologue
## by Bert Villemaire

Winooski's history resounds with evidence of faith, culture and determination. The resiliency of the people of Winooski manifested itself many times over the years: when immigrants introduced language and cultural differences, at the time of the 1927 flood and during mill shutdowns. When many communities throughout Chittenden County began development, Winooski was redeveloping. In 1957, three years after the close of the American Woolen Company mills, citizens in Winooski voted to build a new high school when others spoke of the city becoming a "ghost town."

The greatest piece of this resiliency was the religious faith of the people who persevered against great odds. All churches in Winooski became sources of sharing and caring through the downtimes. Store owners of all faiths left a meal of meat on the soup bone or provided ministers and priests with shoes and clothing for the people in need. Deaths in the community caused an outpouring of support with food and prayer. There was a belief that all would be better if we were patient and let God take charge. Church-centered celebrations marked the calendar throughout the year.

Culture was celebrated beyond the traditional St. Patrick's Day, *Saint-Jean-Baptiste* Day or Christmas. Many Franco-American families gathered on New Year's Day at *"Pepère* and *Memère's"* house. Italians celebrated the birth and christening of children with large family gatherings. Polish weddings were great celebrations. The French language was the focus of the education program at *École St. François Xavier* and at *Couvent St. Louis*. Evolution from child labor to a "go to school and get an education" attitude took place within the entire Winooski culture. Doctors, nurses, lawyers, teachers, priests and nuns, more than enough to support the needs of the community, came from many large families. People overcame the fear of other cultures and mixed over time to form a solid community without losing their cultural identity.

The grit of the mill worker carried Winooski through some difficult times. Slowdowns at the mill created many family difficulties but workers often found ways to overcome these downtimes. It was not uncommon to see laid-off mill workers doing carpentry, plumbing or painting to support their families. Many women did laundry or cleaned houses to help out. In some cases, these jobs continued after people returned to work in the mills. The picture of women slowly walking up Weaver Street after a hot July day in the mill and going home to do more work for their families remains in one's memory. Beyond financial survival, it was a way of life. Young people participated in many activities because of the volunteer effort of many citizens. This spirit of volunteering, giving to others, has been passed down through generations. Fund raising, coaching, mentoring and working at the church bazaars stood as examples of "making it happen despite the odds."

Winooski history is more than a microcosm of American culture. It is a cherished lifestyle full of faith, cultural celebration and a determination to make life better for the next generation.

*Bert Villemaire is Coordinator of Assessment and Instruction at Winooski Middle/High School. He was educated at St. Louis Convent, St. Francis Xavier School, Winooski High School and the University of Vermont. He comes from a local family and has ties to several cultures: a Franco-American father who worked at the mill, an Irish-American mother and an Italian-American wife who grew up in Winooski. Many of the buildings in Winooski hold memories of the mill days, which he has shared with schoolchildren, helping them to understand their community's past.*

# Preface

These writings complement exhibits in the Héritage Winooski Mill Museum located in the Champlain Mill in Winooski, Vermont.

Héritage Winooski, a project of Saint Michael's College, is a cooperative effort of merchants, educators and historians which examines the industrial and cultural heritage of Winooski Falls and Vermont during the nineteenth and twentieth century mill era.

Project partners are the Champlain Mill, Chace Mill, Woolen Mill, Winooski Historical Society, Winooski One Hydroelectric Station, Winooski City Hall, Saint Francis Xavier School and Winooski Public Schools.

Onion River Press, a subsidiary of R.N.M. Inc. dba the Book Rack and Children's Pages, has published this book as a generous match for a grant from Vermont Council on the Humanities under a grant from the National Endowment for the Humanities.

# Introduction

Native *Winoskik* Abenaki people fished near Winooski Falls, and cultivated vegetables and tobacco on nearby flood plains thousands of years before the arrival of European colonists. English settlers began small-scale manufacturing in the 1780s, using waterpower to replace the drudgery of handpower.

Yankee capitalists, seeking to profit from the demand for domestic cloth, built Vermont's first complete woolen factory at Winooski Falls in the mid-1830s. A gristmill and expanding textile mills withstood floods, fires, hard times and the rush of wartime demands. Immigrant workers, often entire families, replaced Yankee farm girls as mill workers.

Technologies changed with the advent of steam engines and hydroelectric power. By 1890, the gristmill stopped milling, unable to compete with new methods. The building was dynamited during the 1927 flood to widen the passage for the high water. Only foundation traces remain at the south end of the Winooski-Burlington bridge; proverbial expressions stemming from the mill and miller of earlier times still linger in our vocabulary.

For a little over a century, nearly everyone living in Winooski and in the Chace Mill neighborhood on the Burlington side of the river had some connection with the mills. Mill shut-downs meant hard times for the workers and local businesses.

The writings of local historians in this collection examine the industrial revolution at the Falls from its inception until its final years in the mid-1950s. The recollections of townspeople who lived during the twentieth century mill years describe life, work and diverse cultures in a community dominated by the American Woolen Company, the biggest producer of woolens and worsteds in the United States. Commentaries on mills and river ecology, waterpower technology, and mill building restoration complement these contributions.

This book is a collective effort of many people. The essays and oral histories relate to exhibits in the Héritage Winooski Mill Museum which is located in the renovated Champlain Mill in Winooski, Vermont.

*Laura Krawitt*

# SECTION ONE

# Winooski Falls

# The Abenaki and the Winooski
## *by Frederick M. Wiseman*

The Abenaki people are part of the Wabanaki Confederacy, a group of closely related native American peoples inhabiting the lands from Cape Breton Island, Nova Scotia to the Lake Champlain Valley. The people called by anthropologists "the Western Abenaki" were the inhabitants of what is now called the Winooski Valley and its environs. Interestingly, the town of Winooski is one of the few place-names still remaining in Vermont with its old Western Abenaki name *Winos* (wild leek) *-ik* (place). There have been many *"Winoskik"* villages of the Abenaki stretching back in time to what archaeologists call the Archaic Period, several thousand years before Christ. Vermonters have a fascination with the Abenaki past, and the artifacts found or quarried by amateur or professional collectors, now housed in Vermont museums, attest to the Abenaki presence in the valley.

The village of Winooski was also known to and reported by early French traders, diplomats and missionaries who saw the native Winooski people in the early seventeenth century. The *Winoskik* Abenaki people congregated in the "intervale" for spring fishing, especially at the *"namaskik"* or fish place that is now called the Salmon Hole.[1] Not only salmon, but walleyed pike, sturgeon and many other fish congregated there to be harvested with nets, fish traps and special three-pronged fish-spears. Following the fish harvest, the intervale valley was an excellent place to grow corn, beans, squash and tobacco. The yearly flooding of the river, now tightly controlled, gave the crops renewed fertile soil year after year. After the fall harvest, the Winooski people dispersed up the river to hunting camps, returning to the main village for the winter. The coming of maple sugaring heralded the spring fish run and the cycle continued.

After the British Americans took over the Winooski Valley in the

Abenaki fish-spear. *(Based on Dr. Wiseman's replica artifact)*

1700s it was not good to be seen as "Indian," so as in many other communities,[2] the *Winoskik* people faded into historical obscurity by merging with the French community while keeping their culture, history and language intact. The Abenaki were known as "gypsies" or "river rats" in the 1800s, and became important parts of the Euroamerican economy as sporting guides, medicine women, basket, canoe, and snowshoe makers, as well as pursuing "European" occupations. The Abenaki were involved with the nineteenth-century mills in many ways, from producing baskets and cooperage bought by the mills to working on the "line" at the mills. But in this they were little different than other working-class people exploited by the mill owners during this time.

The *Winoskik* families were mostly ignored by their Winooski neighbors and left alone to keep their culture alive (but hidden) until the 1920s. The Vermont Eugenics Survey[3] and the State of Vermont sterilization program, begun in 1931, targeted many Abenaki families, including those of the Winooski Valley. This genocide[4] drove the Abenaki further underground rather than chance being driven from their homes, and ended "Indian guiding" and the production of "Indian baskets" heretofore often seen for sale in the Burlington area.

It wasn't until the civil rights movement, beginning in the 1950s, and its "red power" offshoot, that native people in Winooski were able to begin reasserting their identity. They had had little concern about their Irish and Franco-American neighbors, but feared those of English descent. They preferred that Swanton and other northwestern Vermont towns lead the way to recognition by the Vermont community. Today, old *Winoskik* families are members of various native organizations in Vermont and attend powwows and traditional gatherings. There are *Winoskik* families on Burlington's Old North End bluffs overlooking the intervale, just as they have

Traditional Abenaki canoe *(Redrawn from photo of Dr. Wiseman's scale model)*

Salmon Hole at Winooski Falls c.1890. (*Courtesy of Special Collections, University of Vermont Libraries*)

for thousands of years. *Winoskik* fisherfolk still catch their fish in the spring, sometimes in defiance of European-based regulations regarding "sport-fishing." *Winoskik* has always been here and it will continue to be.

*Frederick M. Wiseman's family is from Missiquoi (Swanton, Vermont), where he is a member of the Abenaki Nation and director of the Abenaki Tribal Museum and Cultural Center. He received his doctorate in paleoenvironmental studies and archaeology at the University of Arizona. He has taught at Louisana State University and served as a research scientist at MIT. Currently, he is a professor of humanities at Johnson State College.*

# Damn the Dams: The Impact of Dams on Streams
*by Daniel Bean*

A March 1999 *Burlington Free Press* article highlighted the return of salmon to the Connecticut River, after decades of no salmon returns. Why did salmon stop "running" the Connecticut, the Winooski, and other New England rivers? Why and how did they return? Although there were a variety of reasons for the loss of salmon runs, the principal one was the construction of dams, which prevented the returning salmon from reaching their home spawning streams in Vermont and New Hampshire. Other reasons include deforestation and over-farming, followed by the silting over of streambeds and exposure of the streams to the heating effect of sunlight. These conditions produced less-than-ideal stream conditions for spawning salmon and other fish. But what are "ideal" stream conditions, and just what impact do dams have on such streams? Where did today's salmon come from? Have stream conditions returned to an "ideal" state? Are the dams gone?

When considering whether a stream might be an ideal stream capable of maintaining a varied and productive fauna, it is helpful to recall those conditions which existed in the past when all of our streams were "natural" and pristine. A natural, well-balanced stream should have good tree cover along its banks to shade and reduce heating by the sun and to help reduce erosion by action of the roots holding the stream bank; cool temperatures (57°F is ideal for trout streams); high dissolved oxygen concentrations (above 8 ppm); little or no silting of the bottom; a varied bottom of gravel or stones; ripples and pools with good flow rates; low or no fecal bacteria; medium hardness which provides a good buffer against

This crib dam, c.1876, still remains upstream of the dam built in 1992 at Winooski Falls. It is one of the earliest dams using concrete as crib fill. *(Courtesy of Winooski One Partnership)*

acid rain or natural organic acids from decomposition in the soil; low total dissolved solids; low nutrient values for phosphate and nitrate; low organic load; and a varied fauna.[1]

Any changes in a natural stream's physical characteristics are apt to have deleterious impacts on its water quality. Deforestation of the stream bank by farming or logging would increase erosion, silting, temperature, rate of run-off after rains and nutrient loading. It would also change the characteristics of the bottom (silt over rocks), and reduce the complexity of the bottom insect community. The Quebec Lakes Program encourages the use of natural cover along lake edges and streams, even by providing the plants to homeowners.

Bridge and road construction could have short-term and long-term impacts. During construction there is disruption of the stream bottom and, oftentimes, permanent change by the addition of large rubble to prevent erosion. Frequently a river might even be moved entirely out of its original riverbed to "improve" flow (channeling). Salt spread on roads during winter could also make its way to nearby streams.

Poor farming practices often increase nutrient loading and silting, and add bacteria. Plowing too close to a stream edge removes a natural buffer zone which helps slow soil run-off. It also may hasten loss of streamside trees by cutting roots and water supply. Winter manuring, or manuring during wet spring rains, particularly in fields adjacent to streams, results in the direct and often massive introduction of organic wastes and bacteria into the stream.

Dams which impound water increase silting in their holding pools, eventually filling in and requiring dredging to maintain their capacity. The impounded water also provides a warming time for the surface waters and reduces downstream flow. Conversely, such dams can provide for continual summer flow during dry spells by gradual release of the water. The Tennessee Valley Authority lakes are famous for the cool water they provide to below-dam trout streams. The dams are deep enough so that the water becomes stratified, with the warmer water at the surface and the colder water near the bottom. The dams release the cold, deeper waters. On rivers used by spawning salmon, the dams also stop such runs and, after about four or five years, can eliminate natural salmon from those streams. This occurred in the Winooski River after the construction of a dam in 1830.

Home construction resulting in streamside lawns can have deleterious run-off. Lawn fertilizer increases the nutrient load; lawn pesticides kill stream fauna. Over time, a well-fertilized lakeside or streamside lawn produces an overgrown lakeside water zone.

Waste disposal with increased populations and number of towns and factories can result in high nutrient and waste loads in the streams. Many streams are still used as the receiver of town and individual wastes, either untreated or only partially treated. In the past, with few people, and towns scattered along the waterways, the impact of this practice was minimal.

In some cases both past deleterious changes and subsequent "healing" changes have occurred. For example, as each dam along the Connecticut River came up for its license renewal, efforts were made to have fish ladders or elevators installed to facilitate the salmon's passage around the dam. At the same time New Hampshire, Vermont, and federal fish and wildlife departments were stocking former salmon-spawning streams with young salmon. As the salmon matured and moved downriver, they became imprinted to the scent of their spawning stream. After four or five years of growing at sea, the survivors began returning to these streams. The *Burlington Free Press* article was remarking on the success, albeit limited, of the return of the salmon. It will take years, if ever, for the runs to return to the conditions our forefathers saw, when "you could walk across the river on the backs of the salmon, there were so many!"

In the Winooski River, natural runs ceased in 1830. Vermont started stocking salmon below the lower dam in the early 1970s to provide limited fisheries in that area. With the completion of Winooski One Hydroelectric Station and its fish trap at Winooski Falls, stocking was stopped below the dam and started in upstream brooks. About 20,000 salmon smolts have been stocked each year since 1993. In 1999, fifty-four salmon were captured at the Winooski Falls fish trap, counted, measured, weighed and trucked upstream to spawn. The number of returning salmon has gradually increased; the Department of Fish and Wildlife is optimistic that this trend will continue.

However, bypassing the dams is not the only requirement necessary to return salmon to their streams. Reforestation[2] has been beneficial in improving the water quality. The introduction of good farming practices has also been helpful. With public awareness of the problems and potential solutions, our streams will improve, and dams (both power and flood control) will just be obstacles to canoe travel.

Turning back to the Winooski River, a brief history of human activity at the Winooski Falls area illustrates the impact which can occur. Early French settlers were the first Europeans to arrive. With them came the lumbering of the climax forests[3] of the area, first along the river and later the uplands. The Winooski River was an easy avenue to float the lumber to the lake. But such activity also brought the first stages of bank destruction and erosion. Lumbering continued after the arrival of the English settlers. In the 1780s Ira Allen built the first dam at Winooski Falls, just east of the remains of the Chace Mill dam. This was called the upper dam. This dam, destroyed in the 1830 flood, was rebuilt and lasted until the flood of 1927. In the 1830s a second dam was constructed at the lower falls where Winooski One Hydroelectric Station stands today. Water impounded by this dam was diverted via a canal (hence Winooski's "Canal Street") to a new mill[4] built just west of the present Woolen Mill.

Over time, mills were built, destroyed by fire, rebuilt and enlarged. In 1876 a new timber-crib dam was built at the lower falls. (Part of this dam was discovered during the construction of the hydroelectric station in 1992.) All of this activity, both industrial and damming, had deleterious impacts on the Winooski River in this region (as did construction, industry and farming practices all along the length of the river). Fishing records seem to indicate that either the 1780's Allen dam or the later 1830 dam resulted in the end of migrating salmon. Perhaps this prevented the salmon from experiencing even harsher conditions as development continued.

In the 1880s Winooski's sewage drained directly into the river, as did that of most towns. By the 1890s the river water was so polluted it could no longer be used by the mills for dyeing operations. In 1914 the first municipal sewage system was installed in Winooski. But one problem solved was quickly replaced by others. By the 1920s a carbonizing plant next to the river was reclaiming used wool from rags by a process using sulfuric acid, which was then dumped into the river. Although the Winooski mills did neutralize the acid before it was released into the river, the amount of soda ash they used was not always measured. As someone commented, "those poor fish!" The addition of a coal-fired generating system to increase production resulted in soot belching from the smokestacks. For many years the river turned the color of the day's dyeing (this phenomenon of dyeing streams was still occurring in some Vermont streams well into the 1940s).

However, the salmon were the principal losers because of dam constructions. With the dams blocking their passage upstream to their spawning streams, the fishery, so supportive of the native Indian population prior to the arrival of the Europeans, disappeared. Only by annual stocking by the Department of Fish and Wildlife were salmon able to be fished from the lower Winooski.

In 1992, Winooski One Partnership constructed a new dam at the lower falls. One of many conditions imposed for this project was to install a fish trap to assist upstream migration of salmon and trout. This was done and today visitors can watch as members of the Vermont Fish and Wildlife Department measure, weigh and identify the fish before trucking them upstream and releasing them above the Essex dam. There is hope for the return of a salmon fishery. With stocking, a way around the dams, and the lamprey eel control project (to relieve the adult salmon from the weakening effects of the lamprey strikes) the future looks brighter for both Vermont fish and human river users.

*Daniel Bean, native of Enosburg Falls, Vermont, and graduate of the University of Vermont with a doctorate from the University of Rhode Island, was a biology professor for twenty-nine years at Saint Michael's College. As an ecologist with a specialty in aquatic systems, he spent many years working with teachers on using aquatic systems to teach science. He continues to work with teachers and their students and to advise them via the Internet.*

# SECTION TWO

# A Textile Mill Economy

# Counting Sheep and Other Worldly Goods
### by Jennie G. Versteeg

When we discuss the industrial revolution, we usually mean the social and economic changes that mark the transition from a stable, agricultural and commercial society to a modern, industrial society that relies on complex machinery rather than tools. We are usually referring to Britain in the period from the middle of the eighteenth to the middle of the nineteenth century, but the same changes occurred elsewhere at later times and at different speeds. In U.S. economic history, the theme of industrialization marks in large part the break between the 1815-1850 period and the one before.

What I am going to do here is first touch on the industrial revolution in general and relate it to New England's economic development, specifically her textile industry. This will give us some perspective on Vermont's economic coming of age during a period in which there was an especially rapid rise and fall of the sheep industry.

Dramatic changes in society took place during the industrial revolution as inventions and technological innovations generated a factory system with machine production and division of labor. Workers who used to be employed predominantly in agriculture gathered increasingly in urban factory centers, while agriculture

MERINO PRIZE SHEEP,

The Property of S. Jewett, Esq. Weybridge, Vermont.    See "The Cultivator," for 1846, page 66.

Merino Prize Sheep, Property of S. Jewett, Esq., Weybridge, Vermont, 1846. *(Courtesy of Vermont Historical Society)*

itself also underwent profound technological change. Capitalism appeared on a large scale, and a new type of commercial entrepreneur developed from the old class of merchant adventurers. Factories were not unknown before, of course. For example, the Romans had set up a woolen factory in England as early as 200 b.c.e., and many machines were in use. But these were the exceptions rather than the rule. With the industrial revolution they became the rule. So too, wage labor became the norm and with it economic interdependence; consuming-laboring households became linked to businesses in the system of exchange and specialization we label the market economy.

The industrial revolution did not occur overnight. In fact, some would say it was not a revolution at all but rather a gradual evolution taking several centuries. It followed redefinitions of property rights, population displacement, discovery of the New World, and the flow of precious metals into Europe. It also interacted with dramatic changes in world view, for example, as a result of the Reformation and then later the Enlightenment.

Most of us think of the use of steampower as the pivotal innovation of the industrial revolution occurring with James Watt's improved engine of 1769. The single most important development following it was the rise of the cotton textile industry. Actually, the key innovations that made large-scale textile industry possible occurred over a considerable length of time from John Kay's 1733 invention of the flying shuttle to the 1794 invention of the cotton gin by Eli Whitney in the U.S. During this time more and more integrated machine production arose. With the mechanization of production, cotton textiles came into world prominence and superseded flax and wool textiles for which mechanization and supply hurdles weren't overcome until later. This was true in the U.S. as well as in Britain, especially with the advent of the cotton gin, which made U.S. cotton both an export crop and a raw material for domestic industry.

In England, large quantities of coal and iron in close proximity further stimulated general economic growth and especially the growth of railroads and steamships. These in turn widened the market for manufactured goods. So, too, in the U.S. You probably know about the importance of the iron ore shipped out of Port Henry on the New York side of the lake; and the importance of the railroads and steamships in getting Vermont goods to markets was truly revolutionary. Events in our Lake Champlain region very much parallel the general experience.

In the United States, the 1815-1850 period was the one in which manufacturing clearly outgrew its infancy and reached a self-sustaining level. Before we get to 1815, however, we need to back up. From at least 1789 on, when the first tariff act was passed by Congress, industrialization became the subject of policy debates. For example, while no major tariff changes were made for the next twenty years or so, there was active discussion of infant industry protection, that is, the imposition of customs duties to ward off foreign competition while fledgling industries become established. Alexander Hamilton, for one, advocated such measures in his famous 1792 *Report on Manufactures*. Even so, the 1789 Constitution in no way meant the kind of fundamental change in economics that it did in politics. In fact, up to 1808, the colonial economy continued more or less as it had been. In many ways our nation was characterized by a lack of economic development and change.

Economist Frank Taussig in his classic *Tariff History of the United States* (1967) asserts that this lack of structural economic change was largely due to the expansion and profitability of trade and merchant activity. These, however, slowed abruptly in 1808 with the embargo on trade with England and a doubling of import duties, and 1808 marked a true turning point in the industrial history of the U.S. Exciting Vermont smuggling stories notwith-standing, we were largely cut off from foreign trade. During the 1808-1815 period, the wartime restrictions essentially acted as the equivalent of extreme protectionism. Behind the barriers American industry grew rapidly as substitutes were produced for previously imported goods. This impetus for domestic production applied to Vermont as much as to southern New England.

A few years after hostilities ceased, the new industries began aggressively lobbying for continued duties. Businessmen in New England split on tariff issues. Shippers favored free trade; manufac-turers sought protection. In 1816 a tariff raised duties on crucial commodities, and after 1816 Vermont generally became pro-tariff.

Opinions differ on the real significance of the tariff increases occurring from 1816 through the 1830s, but Taussig asserts that they were not crucial to national industrial development, which would have proceeded in any case. While the initial stimulus of the embargo and war decisively altered the direction of economic development, he argues that subsequent tariff changes came after they had ceased to be essential. This is true for all three of the major industries developing in the first half of the nineteenth century-cotton textiles, woolens, and iron.

Even though the postwar glut of British merchandise, together with financial panic, caused a depression in 1819, the general process of industrialization continued. You can read about this, for example, in Alex Groner's *The History of American Business and Industry*. [The] population nearly doubled between 1820 and 1840, but capital invested in the nation's factories quintupled from $50 million to $250 million, largely from foreign sources. Similarly, between 1819 and 1849, private production income from manufacturing increased from $64 million to $291 million. While this was only about an eighth of total national income from private sources, manufacturing had become the fastest growing segment of the economy. Still, as Groner notes, "it was not until almost 1840 that more goods were produced in the mills than in the homes and shops of America."

Into the 1860s, eighty percent of [the] people lived on farms, which made up half the nation's wealth, and farm production increased enormously due to mechanization and the opening of new lands. Yet the number of manufacturing and construction workers more than doubled between 1820 and 1840, from 350,000 to 790,000. Wages, which had been at about fifty cents a day for unskilled workers in 1800, rose to a dollar a day by 1825, with skilled workers receiving about twice that. Unlike Britain, the industrial revolution was welcomed in the U.S. and there was general interest in any device that could lessen the need for labor.

Industry and agriculture were interdependent, and growth in cotton production is especially interesting as an example of an agricultural commodity which increased in importance as industry grew. From an output of eighty million pounds a year in 1815, it grew to 460 million in 1834. U.S. cotton output then constituted more than half of total world output. By 1850, output was more than one billion pounds per year, flowing not just to New England factories, but also to Britain. From 1830 onward, cotton account- ed for about half of U.S. exports until the Civil War.

One very readable source which details the expansion of the New England textile industry is Steve Dunwell's book, *The Run of the Mill* (Boston, 1978). Dunwell starts well before the 1815-1850 period, continues into the mid-1970s, and includes some wonderful illustrations.

The story of New England textiles is initially one of industrial espionage as know-how was smuggled out of Great Britain and implemented in the U.S. I won't cover the colorful specifics – you'll have to read the Dunwell book for that. Suffice it to say that one Samuel Slater introduced a spinning mill in Rhode Island in 1793. This triggered a veritable "cotton mill fever," and many small mills were set up at various riversides to exploit the new technology which Slater had carried with him to the U.S. These factories employed whole families, and we think of them especially as utilizing child labor under what we would now consider extremely exploitative conditions.

Near Boston, however, work had already begun on even more advanced machines and mill designs. By 1813 or so, various versions of power looms had become accepted and were operating in England after initial violence and opposition by workers. Again stealing British machinery know-how, the exportation of which was strictly prohibited, a version of the power loom was introduced in this country, most notably by Francis Cabot Lowell (1775-1817), whose Boston Manufacturing Co. Inc. was born in Waltham in 1813. By early 1815, the company was running the first fully integrated factory in the United States, using a single power loom, carding engines, and spinning machines.

One important aspect of the Waltham system and its power looms was that it needed different labor than the Slater system mills. Intelligence and dexterity were required but not necessarily strength. Young women became the preferred workers for power looms, whereas they had been rejected on economic grounds by Slater. If we think of illustrations of this era, typically the workers portrayed are young women, prim and properly attired, carefully tending their machines.

This then becomes the period we associate with large numbers of northern New England farm girls moving south to the mills, where they lived in supervised boarding houses and at night wrote poetry and letters and went to uplifting talks. We think of Lowell, Massachusetts especially, which was developed after the death of Francis Cabot Lowell with the 1822 establishment of the Merrimack Manufacturing Co. Lowell became the best known of the integrated factory towns, but there were competing textile centers, for example, in Chicopee, Manchester, and Nashua.

The average stay of young women workers at the mills seems to have been around three years, during which time they acquired some cash, assisted in paying off mortgages on the family farms, sent brothers to college, and

"... for those who throw / The clanking shuttle to and fro, ..."
*(Illustration by Winslow Homer for William Cullen Bryant's* The Song of the Sower, *1881)*

gained a taste for independence. The letters of the mill girls make interesting reading as they described their experiences for the folks back home. Two books you might like to look at are *Farm to Factory: Women's Letters 1830-1860*, edited by Thomas Dublin (New York, 1981), and the collection edited by Benita Eisler, *The Lowell Offering: Writings by New England Mill Women, 1840-1845* (Philadelphia, 1977). Here is part of a December 1945 letter that appears in the Dublin book, written by a woman who intermittently worked in the mills for about two years before returning to Vermont:

> Perhaps you would like something about our regulations about going in and coming out of the mill. At 5 o'clock in the morning the bell rings for the folks to get up and get breakfast. At half past six it rings for the girls to get up and at seven they are called into the mill. At half past 12 we have dinner, are called back again at one, and stay till half past seven . . . . I think that the factory is the best place for me and if any girl wants employment, I advise them to come to Lowell. (104)

In fact, by this time Lowell has experienced its first labor unrest, appeals for better conditions and shorter hours (a ten-hour day was desired). Most sources seem to suggest that living and working conditions initially faced by the women in the mills were no worse than the hard, physical labor, lack of privacy, and overcrowded conditions facing them back home. But by the late 1830s reports of deteriorating conditions, including speedups, VD among mill girls, and other problems proliferate. Employer attitudes toward workers have changed by then, too. Consider the following 1855 opinion:

> As for myself , I regard my work people just as I regard my machinery. So long as they can do my work for what I choose to pay them, I keep them, getting out of them all I can. What they do or how they fare out-side my walls , I don't know, nor do I consider it my business to know. They must look out for themselves as I do for myself. When my machines get old and useless, I reject them and get new, and these people are part of my machinery. (Dunwell, 101)

Here is a real capitalist speaking! Things had come a long way from Lowell's founding as a model community of paternalistically regulated boarding houses, strict attention to propriety and the moral character of young farm women, and planned cultural activities.

Eventually, with so many new factories, the mills faced labor shortages, and recruiting new workers became more difficult. Labor contractors were used to recruit women from further and further north. Ultimately, of course, immigrants provided a solution to this shortage, and their numbers climbed dramatically from 8,000 in 1820 to 23,000 in 1830, 84,000 in 1840, and then 370,000 in 1850.

The Irish formed the first immigrant wave. Irish families often settled in shantytowns at the outskirts of the mill towns. Initially they did construction work at the mills. Railroad work also became important from the mid-1830s as by 1835 the Lowell-Boston railroad, for example, was in place. Attitudes toward the immigrants were mixed at best, foreshadowing later immigration restraints.

Besides immigration, other population shifts occurred as well in this period, for example, urbanization and westward migration. In 1820, only 700,000 people out of a total population of 7.9 million lived in urban settlements; by 1850, this had grown to 3.5 million out of the then total population of 19.6 million. Whereas in 1820 only twenty-seven percent of the population lived west of the Alleghenies, by 1850 this had climbed to forty-five percent.

Also, let's not forget that many technological changes occurred besides those in textiles. This period is rich in inventions and innovations, ranging from the cast-iron plow developed in 1819, to machine tools and calico printing in the 1820s, improved turbines, mechanical reapers, the repeating pistol, the thresher, and the telegraph in the 1830s, the steel plow, carpet looms and patterned weaving, the sewing machine, an improved steam engine, and the safety pin in the 1840s. Things like upright rotary knitting machines and greater steel availability came in the 1850s. By 1850 more than 2,500 patents were being granted each year. At the same time, steam as an energy source continued to make gains. Steampower and waterpower had coexisted since the 1820s, competed equally from the 1840s on, and then after the Civil War steam mills became dominant.

Once mechanization and integrated production had achieved mass-production levels, and supply problems had been solved, economic activity became vulnerable to demand swings and fluctuations in raw material prices. Indeed, periodic downturns became a reality with which entrepreneurs had to contend as depressions came with great regularity in 1827, 1837, 1848, 1857. Gradually the advantages of bigness and capital reserves as a mechanism for survival became clearer. Already in the panic of 1819, the larger Waltham-type mills survived better than the ones of the smaller, Rhode Island-type.

Now, what was going on in Vermont meanwhile? For one thing, you'll have noticed by now that I have still not touched on woolens and sheep, though that's what we associate with Vermont, and sheep are mentioned in my title. In fact, I have saved wool and sheep as a transition to Vermont and the Champlain Valley.

In the American colonies, sheep raising started in Jamestown in 1607. There were stringent English laws against exporting wool in an attempt to make the colonists use English cloth. Early on, this drove the settlers to raise sheep here. George Washington, for example, imported sheep and brought spinners and weavers from England. But generally during the 1700s sheep raising and wool production were small in scale and domestic in purpose.

Spinning and weaving were early established in New England, at first in homes, later in small factories, and the first factory in America to use waterpower to weave wool was established in 1788 at Hartford, Connecticut. It was encouraged by tax exemption and a bounty on each yard woven. Also encouraging was the importation into Connecticut of a large flock of merino sheep in 1802. This was followed by thousands more in 1809-10, when Vermont's Colonel William Jarvis of Weathersfield played a key role. In Rhode Island in 1810, carding and spinning by machine began in an older cotton mill, and woolen production increased. Overall, woolens grew from a $4 million industry in 1810 to one of $19 million by 1815.

Still, it was overshadowed by the cotton industry. For one thing, the technology of wool manufacturing was much slower to move out of the home than cottons. It improved in the 1830s when the different production steps – cleaning, spinning, weaving and finishing – were united in a single industry. A condenser, combining a group of carding machines, was developed in 1826; a burr-picking machine to clean wool came in 1834. The other major obstacle, that of deficient supply and poor quality wool, also was solved by the 1830s with the growth of the merino sheep industry. Let me call your attention to an interesting piece on the Vermont sheep industry: Suzanne Duncan's 1986 Middlebury College senior thesis, "The Role of the Merino in the Sheep and Woolen Industries of Vermont." Thanks to the annual Nuquist Award competition sponsored by the Center for Research on Vermont, you can find it in Special Collections at the University of Vermont.

Of the four hundred merinos Jarvis imported to Weathersfield, some made it to the Champlain Valley, specifically Shoreham in Addison County, in 1816. Merinos became a craze and subject to inflation and speculation as they arrived at a time of steadily increasing demand for wool. The rise in the price of these finely woolled sheep was dramatic indeed: "In 1809 the value of a pure Merino ram was anywhere from one thousand to fifteen hundred dollars," reports Duncan (35). This was not only true in Vermont but in Connecticut and elsewhere, too.

The initial high prices certainly were an incentive to import more sheep and during the 1810-11 period some 20,000 additional merinos were brought into the U.S. The general speculative craze for sheep couldn't last, of course, and by 1813 in Vermont the results of Jarvis's importations were beginning to be felt. Prices dropped until the value of a ram in 1815 was about a dollar. Lower prices in turn were taken advantage of by additional buyers.

The growth in sheep was supported by the growth in the woolen mills in southern New England, which, if you remember, had previously suffered from a lack of good wool. By 1840 Vermont had 1,681,000 sheep, and by 1845 this had climbed to our peak of more than six million. At the same time, the quality of fleeces produced improved dramatically as merinos were crossbred with domestic breeds, increasing the weight per fleece. In 1812, the yield of Vermont's best rams, for example, was six percent wool to body weight; by 1844 it was fifteen percent (Duncan, 45).

Once there was such an abundance of sheep, however, the demand for wool had to be stable, or farmers were hurt. This generated increased pressure for protectionism, coinciding with and following the embargo and War of 1812. The end of the war and reopening of importation of foreign woolen goods were part of what caused the drop in merino prices, of course.

By 1816 the prices of merinos and their wool had bottomed out, but it was not until the 1860s that they would equal their earlier highs. By then, Vermont had gone through a phase where wool was its dominant product in the 1830s and 1840s, to a phase of breeding merinos for the western trade in the 1850s. By 1850 the number of sheep in Vermont had dropped to 1,014,122, yielding 3.4 million pounds of wool, while Ohio became the single largest sheep breeding state. Thus, we really are talking about a rather rapid rise and decline. And the drop didn't stop in 1850. As Census of Agriculture data reveal, Vermont had 296,576 sheep in 1900 and by 1945 just 15,459.

The timing of the sheep craze was fortunate for Vermont. As Duncan explains: "The production of wheat had begun to decline in the early 1820s and by 1827-28, the wheat crop had experienced irreparable damage." Wheat flour had been a major export product of the U.S. from early on, and during the 1797-1810 years wheat had been Vermont's staple crop. Wartime demand raised prices, and the crop remained profitable despite restrictions. However, 1817 was the last year of such profits, and Vermont farmers experienced insect problems, rust, and frost the next several seasons. Besides, the market for wheat may well have been overcrowded by then. The new staple, sheep, thus replaced the declining one.

Other things were also going on in this period in the Champlain Valley. For example, there was the transportation revolution with its canals and railroads, urbanization, and the population and income ups-and-downs of various communities. A nice discussion of many of these trends can be found in the collection edited by H.N. Muller III and S.B. Hand, *In A State of Nature*, which has wonderful data in the appendices as well as reprints of articles (Montpelier, 1985).

The question of where in Vermont people settled, is shown in figures in *In A State of Nature*, specifically in Appendix B, and is discussed also in a piece by T.D. Seymour Bassett, "The Leading Villages of Vermont in 1840." The observed settlement patterns and growth are linked, of course, to the transportation revolution as well as to the gradual, northward pushing back of frontiers. The change in Burlington, especially, is dealt with by Bassett, and with that the concentration of banking and other activities. In general, urbanization continued as more of the population became concentrated in the leading communities.

Even in agriculture we should remember, as Edwin Rozwenc reminds us in "Agriculture and Politics in the Vermont Tradition," another piece reprinted in *In A State of Nature*, "The 'sheep mania' had never, by any means, turned Vermont into a series of sheep pastures. The older patterns of diversity, associated with the age of self-sufficiency in Vermont agriculture, continued." In the 1840s and 1850s Vermont still produced more than 500,000 bushels of wheat, two million bushels of corn, and more than that of oats. Yet outputs of wheat, corn, beef cattle, and pork were dropping as western competition increased.

In this period, the only consistent increase, says Rozwenc, "was in the number of milk cows and the production of dairy products, already portending the development of Vermont as the great dairy state of New England." In 1850 there were some 146,000 milk cows in the state, and by 1860 there were almost 175,000 as the coming of the railroad made it feasible for Vermont dairy products to be sold in Boston and New York. By this time the lake region had seen a profound change in agriculture. Specialization and commercialization had occurred, and with these came more legislative action on behalf of agriculture. Woolens profited from the cotton disruptions of the Civil War, while the textile machine shops converted to arms manufacture.

By the mid-1800s Vermont had come of age. The Champlain Valley had been integrated into the national economy and shared the nation's growth patterns and its prosperity. Alas, it was also vulnerable to national depressions, and as the sheep industry demonstrates, subject to the virtual disappearance of whole industries due to activity totally beyond state control.

"Counting Sheep and Other Worldly Goods," is reprinted from *Lake Champlain: Reflections on Our Past* edited by Jennie G. Versteeg (Burlington: University of Vermont, 1989) with permission from the Center for Research on Vermont, 589 Main St., UVM, Burlington VT 05401-3439. Copies available. Email crv@uvm.edu or call 802-656-4389.

*Dr. Jennie G. Versteeg has, since 1974, participated in numerous Vermont history projects, including those of the Center for Research on Vermont, University of Vermont. Until 1996 she was professor of economics at Saint Michael's College, specializing in international economics and Canadian Studies. Since 1996 she has been working in project and performance management as a senior consultant and lead instructor with The Business Consulting Group, Inc. of Ottawa, Canada.*

# Industrial Growth in Winooski
## *by David J. Blow*

### Harnessing the Winooski

Ira Allen made the first attempts to harness the waterpower of the Winooski River at the present site of the City of Winooski for the elementary needs of settlers. He built a grist and saw mill there in the last decades of the 18th century. In 1802 Amos Weeks applied the waterpower to a more specialized enterprise - manufacturing cloth. He built a small establishment for the fulling and finishing of cloth at the south end of the present bridge. Little is known about Weeks personally except that he died in 1814 at the age of thirty-four.

The major processes in the manufacture of woolen cloth were scouring, picking, carding, spinning, warping, weaving, fulling, washing, dyeing, napping and shearing.

The purpose of the fulling operation was to shrink and strengthen the loosely woven cloth as it came from the loom and to remove the grease that was added after scouring to reduce static electricity. Before the development of the rotary fulling mill in the 1830's there were two types of water power fulling mills: one had a vertical action and the other horizontal.

**The Manufacture of Woolen Cloth**

Scouring removes grease and dirt.

Carding straightens fibers.

Spinning twists fibers into yarn.
*(From* Cyclopedia of Textile Work, *Vol. II, 1915)*

Weaving alternates yarns to make cloth.
(From Draper High-Speed Looms, 1948)

Fulling shrinks and strengthens cloth.
(From Cyclopedia of Textile Work, Vol. VII, 1915)

In the former, the one used by Weeks, two or more large wooden hammers were alternately raised and dropped by cams attached to the shaft of the water wheel. The hammers struck the cloth that was soaking in a trough of water to which a fulling solution of soap and other agents had been added. In the latter type, the hammers were pushed against the cloth. The vertical mill produced a heavier fulling action.

It was because the fulling and finishing process required power-driven machinery, special tools or skills beyond the possibility of household manufacture that they became a specialized business early.

Amos Weeks not only used the water of the Winooski River to full cloth but also to card. This was the third step in the manufacture of wool cloth; it followed the washing of the raw wool [after picking, i.e., loosening the matted washed wool]. The purpose of carding was to straighten and intermix the wool fibers.

The early carding machines were wooden cylinders which were held in a frame and covered with "card clothing," leather in which were inserted bent wire bristles. The wool was carried around on the clothed surface of the rotating main cylinder while a smaller cylinder worked against it and combed it. The carding machine was a great time-saver and produced a much finer and more uniform "carding" than the hand process. Its introduction caused the speedy disappearance of the process from the home.

The brief history of Weeks' enterprise can be traced in several advertisements in the local Burlington newspaper. These notices were similar to those of other businessmen of the period who were seeking either trade, help or payments. In 1806 Weeks announced:

### Carding at Onion River Falls

The public are notified that the carding machine is in good order and completely repaired with new cards and will be tended by a person, who from long experience, has given general satisfaction.

Vermont Centinel *July 2, 1806*

On August 20th of that same year Weeks bought out his partner and the deed gives us some idea of the establishment. For the nominal consideration of one dollar, Amos Weeks purchased from Samuel Fletcher of Shelburne all his right and title to:

"One shop situated in Burlington at Onion River Lower Falls, also situated at the same place, two carding machines, one fulling mill, wood to a clothier's press, two dye kettles."

"Also one dwelling house occupied, at said Falls; all of which property the said Fletcher and Weeks have hithertofore held and claimed in partnership."

By September of 1806 Amos Weeks' business had expanded to dyeing and [he had] opened a mill at Essex.

### Cloth Dressing

The subscriber informs his old customers and the public in general that he has received a supply of dye stuffs and commenced dressing cloth at his old stand in Burlington. All colors dyed and dressed on the shortest notice. Scarlet colors as usual.

He would likewise inform his friends the public, that his carding machines are in operation both at Burlington and Essex where carding is done on the shortest notice; good roles are warranted, if the wool is well picked and greased. Amos Weeks

Vermont Centinel *Sept. 3, 1806*

Further expansion is indicated in the purchase of more land by Weeks from Moses Catlin in 1807. The contents of the deed give a good description of the enlarged factory and the circumstances under which it was run.

. . . the land now occupied by the building owned and occupied by

Amos Weeks as a clothier's shop - carding works and fulling mill at the falls on Onion River where at said Catlin's mills now stand, with sufficient room about said building to store or lay up such quantity of wood from time to time as may be necessary to carry on said business with advantage and sufficient to pass to and from said building and room for the convenience of tenter bars to dry cloth dressed at said works and the privilege of taking sufficient water from the floom or dam of said Moses Catlin for the use of said business. . .

It would seem from the above that Weeks had previously leased land from Catlin or had only a verbal agreement. A year later the business was further enlarged to include an oil mill. Again in October of 1808 we find advertised in the local paper:

". . . a machine for shearing cloth in motion by water at his factory at Burlington . . . which shears at the rate off four yards a minute. "

Vermont Centinel *October 7, 1808*

These later additions were optional finishing operations done in these fulling establishments. One was dyeing; another was napping, or the brushing of the fulled cloth by teasels, a variety of thistle, which were held in a wooden frame. Shearing was a highly skilled process of cutting off the raised nap on the cloth with a large pair of shears.

The business continued to be carding and fulling wool in the summer, dressing and dyeing finished cloth in the autumn and winter. There are no records to indicate how much business was actually done or its source. However, the business must have come from Burlington and the farmers of the nearby Chittenden County towns.

In this period of American woolen manufacturing it was the normal course to grow gradually from a carding and fulling mill to a full-fledged factory. During this period the mills supplemented and cooperated with household manufacture. During the thirteen years that Amos Weeks carried on the business there is no evidence that any weaving of cloth was done by machine. It is most likely that this process was still done in the home in this area.

During the War of 1812 there was a small factory making broadcloth in the area of Winooski Falls on the Burlington side. A newspaper described the process but did not state the ownership.

When Amos Weeks died May 22,1814, his manufacturing establishment was taken over by Moses Catlin who leased it to different parties. Finally it was sold to Charles Burnham. By 1820 Burnham was employing four men and producing 7000 yards of flannel cloth per month in addition to the regular business of fulling and carding. He expanded the business in 1827, building a new factory a few rods below his main operation and installing two double carding machines and two more fulling mills. This growing enterprise was wiped out in the flood of 1830 and apparently no effort was made to revive it. Charles Burnham died in 1833.

Such minor ventures gave no permanent industrial character to the community at Winooski Falls. That would fall to their successor, the great woolen mill, built there in the 1830s. They were merely the necessary accompaniment of the economic self-sufficiency common to rural New England in the early 19th century.

## The Industrial Revolution in Winooski

In the last half of the decade of the 1830s a mill was built at Winooski Falls that was the first complete woolen factory in the State of Vermont. Here raw wool was made into cloth in a process performed under one roof. Capital was furnished not by one man nor his family but by a group of men working for both their own interest and that of the community.

On November 10, 1835 Luther Loomis, Samuel Hickok, Henry Moore, Philo Doolittle, Sidney Barlow and Carlos Baxter received a legislative charter as the Burlington Mill Company. They were all Burlington men, merchants, lawyers and capitalists. All of them were vigorous, keen, imaginative and bred in the tradition of enterprise. Doubtless aware of the profits being made in the Massachusetts textile mills, these businessmen were determined to use the water power at Winooski Falls to turn spindles and create a fortune.

It was a considerable undertaking in those days to found a manufacturing concern. It involved the digging of flumes and the damming of the river as well as putting up of the mill itself. A shanty village sprang up in pasture land and the peaceful cross-roads hamlet of Winooski Falls was transformed into a boisterous construction camp. This transformation of the quiet riverbank where Ira Allen had built the schooner "Liberty" marked the most

34

radical change in Winooski's history since the building of Fort Frederick in 1773.

The factory obtained wool locally from farmers in Chittenden County. The company dispatched its finished goods by boat in the summer and in winter shipped them by wagons over the Winooski Turnpike to Boston.

At six o'clock every morning except Sunday, the factory bell sounded the beginning of a long day's work. The hours varied with the season, but usually they lasted from sunrise to sunset with two brief breaks for breakfast and the noon meal. Longer hours were attempted, but the owners preferred to avoid the higher lighting costs. Indeed, considerations of economy, not humanity, reduced the working week from seventy-eight hours in the 1830s to sixty-nine by the end of the 1840s.

The manufacture of broadcloth was commenced in the spring of 1839. The timing could hardly have been worse. Just at the time the new company began to turn out cloth, the market dropped and depression set in. The Burlington Mill Company, capitalized at $200,000, was seriously under-financed. It had spent most of its capital ($130,000) for fixed assets and had to plunge into debt from the start in order to purchase wool and pay salaries and wages.

The employees were green hands with little skill or experience, and the quality of the goods themselves reflected the conditions surrounding their manufacture. A higher standard of perfection had already been attained by foreign manufacturers and the best fabrics in this country were almost all imported from Europe.

The misfortunes and anxieties which so often follow upon the organization of an under-capitalized company weren't spared the Winooski enterprise. The owners seemed unable to secure additional capital. Everyone was dissatisfied with the fact that the factory didn't do better. In the fall of 1840 the company was reorganized, a portion of the stockholders dropping out and the rest assessing themselves some $25,000 to clear off the liabilities and enable them to start square once more.

The compromise tariff of 1833 had provided for gradual reduction of duties until 1842. In the summer of that year the rate reached a low mark of 12½, purely nominal as far as protection was concerned and useful only for revenue. The lower duties on foreign woolens forced American manufacturers like the Winooski factory to sell their cloth for less than the cost of the raw wool.

The Burlington Mill Company lost thousands of dollars a week during this period. Two years after the reorganization of 1840 a committee reported a loss of $19,600 in manufacturing.

During July of 1845 the company was again reorganized and the capital stock reduced to $50,000. Previously it had been owned and controlled locally, but under this reorganization most of the stock was the property of Richardson Burrage & Company of Boston, Massachusetts. James Cook, a veteran of long experience in the mills of Lowell, Massachusetts, was appointed agent.

One of the first things Cook accomplished at Winooski Falls was to replace most of the factory machinery. Rapid improvements in woolen machinery made the value of old mill equipment deteriorate so fast that manufacturers were sometimes forced to abandon their whole outfit and furnish their mills with entirely new machines. This changeover was completed by 1847.

Through Cook's connections new sources of raw material were acquired. Wool was purchased from Ohio and Pennsylvania. During this time the factory purchased 300,000 pounds of wool a year from these markets.

Improvement in machinery and the purchase of a finer grade of wool upgraded the quality of the factory's product. The experience of the operators also helped the company to acquire a high reputation for the goods produced. At fairs in Boston and New York, Cook won gold medals for his black cassimeres or kerseymere (*plain [weave] or twilled [weave] woolen cloth for men's apparel*).

These moves appear to have succeeded, as the mill prospered especially during the Mexican War; but in 1849 the company was in trouble again. On May 22, 1849, the property of the mill was attached and shut down by a lawsuit of Richardson, Burrage & Co., one of the largest stockholders, to satisfy a claim for advances. The details of this suit are unknown, but its consequences were disastrous for the company. Two weeks later the Burlington Mill Company went into receivership. J. & J.H. Peck & Co. of Burlington, James Cook and Harry Bradley took over the attached property with the necessary lease to enable them to control and operate the mill. Eventually the referees of the case gave to Richardson, Burrage & Co. an award of $49,300 and all of the property of the company was to be sold at auction.

In November of 1850, the Burlington Mill Company closed its doors once more, for the last time, many feared. The last meeting of the old company was held in Burlington the following month and James Cook went back to Massachusetts.

This early period of the mill, discouraging as it was, is really typical of the history of most American industrial enterprises in that period of the 19th century. The causes of the failure were attributed, in various committee reports, to inexperience on the part of the managers in manufacturing, foreign competition and a falling tariff, injurious purchases of wool, lack of skill to secure a finish on the goods which should enable them to compete in price with other manufacturers and the want of sufficient authority in the agent of the mill. The last cause was referred to by one of the stockholders in the phrase that the company was "town meetinged to death" — meaning that almost every decision was made by vote of the directors or stockholders and without the concentration of authority necessary for prompt and efficient action.

### Industrial Fluctuations in Winooski

For almost two years following an 1850 lawsuit in which Winooski's woolen mills were unable to satisfy financial claims against the company, the machines stood idle in the big building beside the river. Then on October 20, 1852, the property was sold at auction to Charles L. Harding of Oxford, Mass. for $49,000 (though its assets had been valued at $300,000). One year later Charles sold a fourth interest to each of his younger brothers, after which Charles, George and William went into business as partners.

The Hardings were experienced textile manufacturers. They invested $31,000 in new machines and building repairs, making their total investment $80,000.

They manufactured the finer quality of doeskin cloth exclusively. Doeskin is a firm woolen cloth with a smooth, soft surface which was in great demand for men's wear. It was by all accounts of high quality. Under the Harding management the factory produced 1500 yards per day on sixteen sets of machinery. There were 325 persons employed at the mill at this time, of whom about one-third were women.

The principal competition to their black doeskins came from Germany. That problem was compounded by another, the constant effort by other textile manufacturers to entice away Hardings' experienced workmen with promises of higher wages.

After five years of financially good times, the Panic of 1857 forced the suspension of Hardings' Boston selling house. They sold half a year's output — 270,000 yards — at a serious loss, and the future again looked doubtful.

They were on the point of quitting when a fortunate discovery put new life into their business. Like other manufacturers of the day, they had been using domestic wool,

Winooski Mills, 1890s. *(From* Vermont: Its Resources & Industries, *1899)*

but their interest was drawn to cheaper Argentine "mestiza" wool. This import could be bought for twelve cents a pound when local wool cost sixty-five cents per pound. A serious drawback to its use, however, was the fact that it was filled with the burrs of a South American thistle. These burrs could not be removed by any economical process.

The Hardings experimented with the mestiza and soon developed a crude burr crusher. When the burrs were crushed, they could be simply washed out of the wool. This enabled them to enjoy a competitive advantage until the years just prior to the Civil War when industrial spies discovered their secret. Improved burr crushers were built by inventive engineers elsewhere, but the Hardings met with success in the meantime.

The monthly payroll of the Harding mill amounted to $5,500 during the years 1857-1860 - a sizable sum in those days. Two thousand yards of cloth a day were manufactured from a ton of raw wool. The factory consumed 500 to 600 cords of wood and 800 tons of coal per year, so it meant a considerable injection of outside money into the economy of Chittenden County.

The Civil War brought the beginnings of even greater prosperity for the mill. The two younger Hardings had little faith in the stability of business, and having made comfortable fortunes they sold their interest to Charles. As the war increased in scale and duration, the demand for army cloth became tremendous. Harding turned the entire production of the factory to army blue and in the first ten months of the war showed a profit of $375,000. Even by national standards the woolen mill was becoming a big business.

The Burlington Mill Corporation, a newly-formed Boston corporation, bought the company from Charles Harding in November of 1861. The new corporation sold $200,000 worth of capital stock, one-half of the proceeds going to Harding for his property. He also became an associate with seven owners of the Boston firm.

This change of ownership added a new personality to the affairs of Winooski, a man who was destined to leave his mark upon the history of the manufacturing village. Frederick C. Kennedy was a strong, clearly defined personality; he could not be ignored or overlooked, nor frightened, nor flattered. He had been employed at the mill under the Hardings and with the change in ownership was elected treasurer of the corporation and appointed its agent in Winooski. Through his guidance the mill underwent a program of expansion that spread the buildings over an area of two and one-half acres. By the 1880s the factory used 1,400,000 pounds of wool per year, manufactured about 800,000 yards of cloth and gave employment to 700 people.

F.C. Kennedy, Agent, Burlington Mill Corporation. (From 1899 Winooski Vt)

No break in continuity occurred between the old management and the new, but the feeling of responsibility which the Hardings felt for the well-being of the village and their workers inevitably lessened. Under Kennedy's management Winooski became more typical of southern New England mill towns.

Winooski and the woolen mill prospered together through the ups and downs of business cycles until the end of the century. For more than four years – 1893-1896 and part of 1897 - the United States was tormented by what we would call a major depression. In those days they spoke of the Panic of 1893 and of the hard times which followed. Businesses which had formerly been prosperous went into the red; factories shut down; bankruptcies multiplied; wages were cut; workers lost jobs and year after year faced the recurring nightmare of unemployment. Added to this the Wilson Gorman Tariff of 1894 hit woolen manufacturers quite hard. This tariff placed woolens on the free market for the first time in 30 years.

The effect of all this was felt in Winooski. On February 21, 1898 a bill of complaint was filed in the Federal District Court by the Boston commission house of Sawyer, Manning & Co. against the Winooski factory. The commission house claimed that the company owed over $200,000 of which $150,000 was commercial paper endorsed by Sawyer, Manning & Co. It was further pointed out that paper amounting to $25,000 had come due in February of 1898 and had been dishonored. The Burlington Mill Corporation had to go into bankruptcy.

### Amusements.

## DEDICATION BALL
—AND—
## PROMENADE CONCERT
—AT THE—
## NEW COTTON MILL
—OF THE—
### Burlington Woollen Company,
WINOOSKI, VT.,
Under the management of
### Joseph Sawyer Hose Co., No. 1,
TUESDAY EVENING, JUNE 29, 1880,.
BILL $2.50.
All Vermont Railroads and Lake Steamers will carry for fare one way.
A general invitation to the public is extended.
June 26, d3d

*From* The Daily Free Press and Times, *June 28, 1880.*

The physical plant was turned over to a receiver, B.B. Smalley of Burlington, who ran it until 1901. In this year the American Woolen Company purchased the buildings and equipment and added Winooski to the list of factory towns dominated by the national conglomerate.

The American Woolen Company undertook a major program to modernize and enlarge the newly acquired facilities. Eventually they had floor space amounting to 30,000 square feet and provided for a capacity of 16,500 spindles. This national corporation continued the woolen business in Winooski until 1954 when it moved operations to the South in search of cheaper labor. The closing of the factory doors in that year ended Winooski's era as an industrial community.

This article, reprinted with permission from the publisher, first appeared as a three-part series in *Chittenden* in November and December of 1973, and in January of 1974.

*David J. Blow, former archivist at Special Collections, University of Vermont Libraries, has written extensively about local history. He was a contributing author of* Look Around Burlington, Vermont *and* Look Around Winooski, Vermont. *He has also written about Franco-Americans in Winooski. His most recent publication is* Historic Guide to Burlington Neighborhoods.

# The Fuller's Teasel
## by Peter Hope

Teasels are tall coarse plants with prickly leaves and stems. Before the late 1800s, the spiny heads of teasels were used to brush freshly woven woolen cloth "to bring loose fibers to the surface and raise a soft nap" (Buchanan, 1987). In her book *A Weaver's Garden*, Rita Buchanan writes that no man-made substitute works as well as the fuller's teasel with its flexible hooked spines which gently scratch the cloth, "yielding to irregularities rather than snagging and tugging." Named from the Anglo-Saxon verb *taesan* (to pluck or pull), the fuller's teasel is an ideal natural tool." Buchanan describes the brushing as part of a three-step finishing process consisting of fulling, which involves washing the cloth in warm soapy water to draw the yarns together making a denser and thicker fabric; followed by brushing; and finally trimming the raised nap to a uniform thickness.

Teasel

All the species of teasels found in North America are alien, brought over from Europe. Superficially they look a lot like thistles which botanists have placed in the aster family (Asteraceae). What distinguishes teasels from thistles and puts them in their own family (Dipsacaceae), is that they have four separate stamens, the "male" parts with anthers that bear the pollen. Thistles and most members of the aster family have five stamens that are usually fused together, forming a tube tightly surrounding the pistil, or "female" part of the flower in the center. Another distinction between teasels and thistles is that the leaves of teasels are opposite, meaning that there are usually two leaves attached on opposite sides of the stems. Thistles have just one leaf at each point of attachment to the stem. Also, the prickles on teasel leaves are mostly restricted to the underside of the mid-vein of the leaf, instead of along the edges of the leaves, as on thistles.

Teasels, like thistles, have numerous small white-to-purple flowers packed into dense, somewhat cylindrical heads. Below each little tubular cup-shaped flower is a spiny green bract or leaf-like part that gives the flower head a spiny or bristly look and feel.

It is these bracts that make the teasels useful to fullers. All species of teasels have spike-like bracts sticking out below the flowers. But those of the fuller's teasel (*Dipsacus fullonum*) are more stout and they are hooked, or curved backwards. They are stiff yet flexible, making them perfect for the job. The wild teasel is not useful to fullers because its spiny bracts are "weak and straight, rather than strong and curved" (Buchanan, 1987).

The fuller's teasel was frequently planted, sometimes around mills; in the mid-1800s it was a commercial crop grown in upstate New York (Buchanan, 1987). Apparently this species rarely spreads on its own. The wild teasel (Dipsacus sylvestris) does spread and has become a widespread weed in much of North America. In central New York State it is easy to spot in its preferred habitats along roadsides and wasteground, especially in moist low places (Gleason and Cronquist, 1991).

In Vermont the wild teasel has been collected in the Champlain Valley, mostly in Addison County. To help keep track of what grows where, botanists collect specimens, press them and keep them neatly arranged by family in herbaria. The Pringle Herbarium of the University of Vermont has ten wild teasel specimens found in Vermont in its collection. Of these ten, seven were found in Shoreham, and one each in Addison, Middlebury and Orwell. I once saw wild teasel growing in a moist field beside Dead Creek while canoeing in Addison. The Pringle Herbarium also has specimens from other parts of the United States and other parts of the world. In the United States folder are two specimens of Fuller's teasel (*Dipsacus fullonum*), both of which were collected in California. This makes sense because California's climate is described as Mediterranean, which is the preferred habitat of fuller's teasel.

The teasel heads were collected

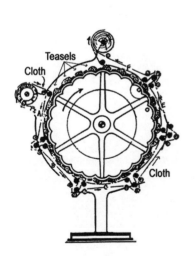

Teasel gig. Dried teasel, mounted on slats in frames on a rotating drum, brush wool cloth to raise the nap. A cylinder holds twenty slats and requires from 2500 to 4000 teasels. Wire brushes have replaced teasels. (*Adapted from* American Wool Handbook, 1948)

and originally fitted into wooden frames with handles. The nap was raised by hand brushing. Later, in water-powered mills after the Industrial Revolution, the heads were put on rotating drums that did the brushing. But by the late 1800s "nearly all the mills began to use wire brushes instead of teasels" (Buchanan, 1987).

*Peter Hope graduated from Middlebury College with a bachelors's degree in anthropology and sociology. Following graduation, he was the program service director at the Vermont Institute of Natural Science in Woodstock, Vermont. He received a master's degree in botany from the University of Vermont. Currently, he is a biology instructor at Saint Michael's College, and president of the Vermont Botanical and Bird Club.*

# Transportation Conditions Affecting
## Winooski Woolen Manufacturing
### *by T. D. Seymour Bassett*

When Burlington capitalists risked some $130,000 to build a woolen mill on the Colchester side of the Winooski River in the late 1830s, superior transportation facilities were one of the favorable conditions which encouraged them to start. Add nearby raw wool, cheap and teachable labor, and most important, abundant waterpower, and the combination produced the leading woolen factory throughout Vermont's textile history.

Burlington was at a major crossing of routes. Throughout history, Lake Champlain provided north, south, and west spokes of the wheel, and the roads north, east, and south the other spokes. Small boats could come up to the Winooski Falls and load woolens for distribution to the thriving communities along the shores of Lake Champlain, but there is no evidence of docks below the falls as there is of docks below Otter Creek falls in Vergennes. This roundabout route was practically never used, except possibly for carrying grain to distant lake windmills before Ira Allen established grist mills at Shelburne Falls and Winooski Falls. Burlington businessmen built the lower road to Winooski, now called Riverside Avenue, to accommodate the new mill. Woolen wagons used it to get to Pearl, Church, and Main streets as the easiest grade to avoid ravine and gully to reach the lakefront.

The Richelieu outlet, with the Chambly lock and canal system completed and refurbished in the 1850s, promised access to Canadian and world markets via the St. Lawrence, as well as access up the river to the Great Lakes. The Northern, or Champlain-Hudson Canal, in its second decade of successful operation, assured the entrepreneurs of an expanding United States market via the Erie Canal and Great Lakes, or by coastal shipping. The canals were repeatedly widened and deepened, but the vision of a ship canal, to make Burlington the center for shipments between New England and the West, was never realized. Like the canals, the wagon roads to the interior of the state, as long as they kept out of the Champlain Valley clay, and bad as they seem by modern standards, were steadily improved and always a notch

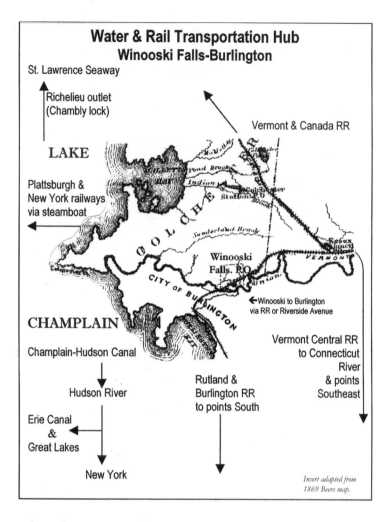

**Water & Rail Transportation Hub**
**Winooski Falls-Burlington**

St. Lawrence Seaway

Richelieu outlet
(Chambly lock)

Vermont & Canada RR

LAKE

Plattsburgh &
New York railways
via steamboat

Winooski
Falls. P.O.

←Winooski to Burlington
via RR or Riverside Avenue

CHAMPLAIN

Champlain-Hudson Canal

Vermont Central RR
to Connecticut
River
& points
Southeast

Hudson River

Rutland &
Burlington RR
to points South

Erie Canal
&
Great Lakes

New York

*Insert adapted from
1869 Beers map.*

better than those nearer the Green Mountains or in the forests of
northeastern Vermont.

Compared to their large, up-to-date competitors in Northfield,
Pownal, and Woodstock, promoters of the Burlington mill were
the closest to the preferred trade routes and the markets they
reached. The Connecticut Valley mills were closer to the Boston
wholesale market, but for at least another decade until the railroads became a reality, the longer water routes could match the
slower land routes.

Local businessmen, aware of the success of railroads in Europe,
were half prepared to fit the freight train into their transport
system. Their vested interest in lake shipping, however, hampered
their efforts to secure a lakeside railroad providing a route to the

West via northern New York or Canada. It was and still is true that water transportation is the cheapest way to ship heavy, bulky freight. But for passengers and fast freight, shipped at higher rates, rails were proving their superiority. Burlington shifted with the times and used the Rutland and Burlington Railroad, with Timothy Follett and Harry Bradley of Burlington among the principal managers, to reach New York more directly than any route via the Vermont Central Railroad. The Rutland's access to Boston via Rutland, Bellows Falls and the Fitchburg line matched the Central's route.

In the few years after 1849, when freight first rolled in Vermont, Burlington found its expected access to the north blocked. Ex-governor Charles Paine, the principal voice in locating the route of the Vermont Central, favored his Northfield interests at the expense of Barre-Montpelier, and put Burlington on a spur, off his main Boston-Montreal route. His Vermont Central also controlled, through the Vermont and Canada Railroad and its Rouses Point Bridge, the connection with the Ogdensburg line across the northern edge of New York. This brought woolens from Northfield and other mills near the Vermont Central by rail to the Great Lakes or to the Ohio Valley in much less time and with fewer transshipments than an all-water route, or even a route using boats as a bridge from Burlington to St. Jean, in Quebec. The Delaware and Hudson Railroad, which could carry lake freight from Plattsburgh, would not have a competing New York-to-Montreal route on the west side of the lake until about 1876.

In 1870, by leasing other lines, including the Rutland, the Central controlled a system reaching from New London to Ogdensburg. This presumably improved the freight situation for the woolen mill until the depression of the 1890s, when the Rutland emerged from the monopoly. It had to build an alternate route north, with a long causeway from Colchester Point to South Hero and through Grand Isle County to the Canadian border, where it connected with a line to Montreal. It finally had its own route to north, this desperate measure providing a second option in the mill's bargaining for better freight rates.

Inferior rail transportation was only one of the reasons the Burlington Woolen Mill had financial troubles from 1844, in spite of pouring in more capital until the total investment reached over $300,000. Once in the hands of Boston capitalists and experienced

Lowell operators the mill survived on innovation (for example, new ways to clean dirty foreign wool), a low-wage, firmly rooted and skilled labor pool, and a government buyer of uniform materials during the Civil War. The wool supply, which had been local and could easily be wagoned to the mill, dwindled, although more slowly in the near parts of the Champlain Valley. The substitution of Argentine wool and other far-off sources increased the import side of the ledger, while the North American rail network put the Winooski mill in wider competition with farther-off factories.

Until the Winooski textile industry ended in the 1950s, the mill received its coal directly on its rail siding and depended on the railroad to ship its product. Better roads, the result of a movement beginning in the 1890s, served the interests of automobiles and trucks, especially after World War I, and provided the flexibility of door-to-door delivery. The highway network, along with plane service from the mid-1930s, although undoubtedly useful for the intercourse between local managers and metropolitan leaders, seems to have had little impact on the mill's shipment practices.

*T.D. Seymour Bassett retired in 1977 as university archivist and curator of the Wilbur Collection of Vermontiana at Special Collections, University of Vermont Libraries. He has written extensively on Vermont social history. He edited* Outsiders Inside Vermont *(1967; 2nd ed., 1976) and* Vermont: A Bibliography of Its History *(1981), and wrote* The Growing Edge: Vermont Villages, 1840-1880 *(1992). His most recent book is* Gods of the Hills, *a history of religion in Vermont to 1900.*

# Yankees and Migrants

# The Methodist Episcopal Church and the Mill Community
## by Linda M. Howe

The Methodists comprise the oldest still-existing congregation in Winooski. When preaching services were held in 1830, Winooski village was a station connected with Burlington. In 1847, the Methodist Troy Conference at Albany, New York organized a separate Winooski station. At first, the congregation held services in homes, schools, and in a rented hall. In spring 1859, members raised a subscription to build its own meeting house. Charles L. and William C. Harding, owners of the the Burlington Woolen Company at that time, donated land on the corner of Follett and West Allen Street "in consideration of one dollar to us paid by the Stewards of the Second Methodist Episcopal Church of the same Colchester located in the Village of Winooski . . . As a further consideration in this deed the Stewards of the Second Methodist Church aforesaid agree to deliver unto the said Charles L. and William C. Harding a deed of three Pews in the Church to be erected on the above described Land. . ." as noted in the Quit-Claims Deed of

Methodist Episcopal Church, Winooski c. 1860. *(From 1899 Winooski Vt)*

"this fifteenth day of October A.D. 1860." In 1860 the church building was completed at a cost of $3,000.

Established by Yankees, this church may have been attended by the Yankee farm girls who came to work in the mill in the early 1840s and lived in the mill boarding house. As in the Waltham System of mill boarding houses in Lowell, Massachusetts, such young women would have been required to attend church weekly. Church records which might have indicated this burned in the 1917 church fire. Minutes from the "M.E. Church" meeting of December 20, 1917 are as follows:

"Meeting of the official board of the M.E. church was held at the parsonage, Monday evening, Dec. 17th, at the call of the pastor to consider business pertaining to the destruction of the church by fire on Sunday, Dec. 16th. (This fire, occurred at about 2:30 and was occasioned by an over-heated furnace which caused the chimney to become so heated as to ignite the wood-work in which it was cased. Inside the partition at this point was more than 12 inches wide. Fire run up the partition into the attic and before the fire engine could reach the scene, the roof was consumed and fallen in.)

Present at the meeting were: Mr. and Mrs. R.H. Washburne, Mr. and Mrs. H.A. Bailey, Mr. and Mrs. S.N. Putnam, Mr. and Mrs. Edgar Bernard, O.W. Edwards, H.E. Bartram, George L. Edwards, W.O. Dyke, F.E. Dandrew, Mrs. F.E. Nash, and C.S. Lord. The pastor reported that the officials of the Congregational church had invited himself and Brothers Bailey and Lord to meet them in Mr. McBride's office shortly after 5 o'clock and while the fire was still burning and they expressed their most sincere sympathy for our church in its great trouble; and made in behalf of their church, the offer of the use of their church at any time for church services, Christmas exercises, socialbles or any other function for as long as we desired.

A vote of appreciation and thanks was passed in response to this invitation and the pastor, The Rev. R.H. Washburne, was instructed to draw up, a suitable resolution, the same also to be published in both the daily papers."

*From Methodist Episcopal archives, courtesy of Bob Beech, lay leader.*

The new church, which cost $10,000, was dedicated on December 22, 1918. There was space allotted for a lecture room and social room as " . . . the church cannot do its full duty to the community without entering the social and intellectual as well as the distinctively religious life of the people."

Methodist Episcopal Church, Winooski c.1972. The church has since been painted dark green, in keeping with the dark color of the original church. *(From* Look Around Winooski, Vermont, *with permission of Chittenden County Historical Society)*

Local missionary projects included programs for the soldiers at Fort Ethan Allen and classes for citizens who did not speak English. The congregation might have realized the need to provide English instruction for foreign immigrants who had come to Winooski for employment in the mills.

The Methodist church has always embraced diversity. The

Methodist Episcopal Church Interior, c. 1860. *(From Consuelo N. Bailey papers, courtesy of Special Collections, University of Vermont Libraries)*

oldest member of the congregation, Elaine Harwood, an Afro-American born in 1898, joined the Winooski congregation in 1915. Mary Elizabeth Hatcher, born in 1915 to an Afro-American couple, Willis J. and Mary Jane (Ward) Hatcher, married Nicodemous McCollum, Jr. They had five children. The McCollum family has remained active in the church to this day. The congregation continues to reflect the increasing racial and cultural diversity of the community with Caucasians, Afro-Americans and Asians among its members. The church remains committed to reaching out to the community and to providing services and facilities for groups seeking to improve the quality of their lives through a closer relationship with God.

*Linda M. Howe is secretary of the Winooski United Methodist Church and a University of Vermont Extension System educator. She is currently pursuing a doctorate in education at the University of Vermont. She lives in Winooski in a brick farmhouse built in the mid-1800s. Her farmhouse, listed on the State Historic Register, was once on Francis LeClair's horse farm.*

# French Canadian Émigrés and Industrialization
*Excerpts from "Emigrés and Industrialization: French Canadians in Burlington and Colchester, Vermont, 1850-1870" by Betsy Beattie*

French Canadian immigrants living in Burlington and Winooski, Vermont in 1850 had probably traveled fewer than two hundred miles to their new home. Most of those who emigrated from Quebec in the first half of the nineteenth century came from the Montreal district of the province, many from the valley of the Richelieu River which flows directly out of Lake Champlain.[1] The physical distance they traveled was short, the time involved usually a matter of days.[2]

The cultural distance they traveled was enormous. Vermont's traditions of freehold land tenure, Protestantism and democracy were a world apart from the centuries-old institutions and the history of French Canada. The mentality of *Québécois* immigrants was an outgrowth of a unique cultural heritage; their behavior was a product of the interplay of old attitudes and new experiences. Any real understanding of the French Canadians in the Burlington area must begin two hundred miles north, in the Quebec they left behind.

After 1803 the French-speaking residents of Canada were all that remained of a once extensive French presence in North America. They and their institutions were vestiges of the *Ancien Régime* now gone not only from the New World but from France as well. That the laws, religion and social organization of New France still existed at all in Canada by the 1800s was the result of the perspicacity of early English colonial administrators who realized that governing the French population they had conquered in 1760 would require the cooperation of those they considered the leaders of that population: the clergy and the *seigneurs* (large land-holders). These two groups, who had formed the elite of New France, were committed to the preservation of the old French institutions which had given them status and authority. The British government soon realized that the clergy and *seigneurs* would be willing to ensure the peaceful cooperation of the French population with their new English rulers in return for English protection of traditional social and legal structures. Accordingly, in the Quebec Act of 1774, the English Parliament sanctioned the continuation of French law, religion, and custom.[3] . . . Preserving their national heritage in the face of English dominance became a paramount goal, one they appropriately labeled *La Survivance* – survival.

At mid-century, the future of the French language and culture in Canada seemed secure. For a large number of French Canadians, however, *La Survivance* alone could not alleviate the grim economic conditions they faced: too many people on too little and unproductive land. Migration off the *seigneuries* (land grants) continued unchecked during the 1830s and 1840s as young men followed the timber trade into the Ottawa River valley and whole families set out in search of usable land. Some *habitants* [settlers] tried squatting on Township lands only to confront the ire and resistance of the English settlers.[4] Others – a few at first, then a growing stream began crossing the border into the United States.

French Canadian migration from Canada to the United States was not an entirely new phenomenon by 1830 or even by 1800. Political upheavals had produced bands of *Québécois émigrés* since the days of the American Revolutionary War and continued to send exiles southward into the nineteenth century. The first to arrive were those French Canadians who had offered assistance to the American Continental Army in its unsuccessful attempt to take Quebec from the British.[5] . . . In succeeding years, around three hundred French Canadians fled the harsh anti-French policies of Governor James Craig (1807-1811) and settled in the Champlain Valley of Vermont.[6] . . .

Political exiles only accounted for a small percentage of those French Canadians who migrated to the United States. Economic distress was a far more common motivation. For many landless *habitants*, especially the young, finding employment was the critical concern, and in the early nineteenth century employment opportunities were far more plentiful in the United States than in any part of British North America. The American-Canadian border was completely open; there were no restrictions on how many could come into the country nor how long they could stay.[7] Furthermore, natural waterways, canals, and, later, railroads linked the two regions and made north-south travel fairly easy.[8] As the century progressed, the United States became an increasingly powerful magnet for the uprooted and opportunistic French Canadian.

Some – the more adventurous, those with more ready cash, those hoping to find farmland – journeyed into the American Midwest.[9]. . . Still, many of the landless, single or with families, found the journey to the Midwest either too costly or too final. It was far cheaper and less painful to head for northern New England and upstate New York, look for work, and hope to return to Quebec in a year or two with enough money to pay off farm debts or buy land.[10] Job opportunities, especially of a seasonal nature, were plentiful. Many farms needed an extra hand for haying or at harvest time. Railroad construction attracted migrant labor. Lumber and brick yards, kept busy by expanding demand for building materials in growing cities and towns, welcomed new workers. Men with carpentry and masonry skills found construction jobs there as well.[11] The simple economic forces of supply and demand were at work; over-populated rural Quebec was sending its surplus manpower to labor-hungry, industrializing New England.

As the agriculture and demographic crises deepened in Quebec, emigration increased. Success stories abounded – some genuine, some exaggerated. Typically, the word of better opportunity spread when a young *saisonnier* or seasonal worker, returned to his rural parish after completing a year's work in the United States. Clad in a new suit of clothes, coins jangling in his pocket, he represented just what the struggling *habitant* lacked: ready cash to spend as he wished and the freedom to travel. Soon friends and relatives would follow, find work, and return themselves, and the cycle would repeat itself.[12]

Sometimes whole families emigrated to look for a new farm or just to seek employment for all able-bodied members. The goals were always the same: to earn money, enough to live on and perhaps enough to save in order to return to the land and life they had known. By the 1840s, 40,000 French Canadians had left Canada.[13] Both the Church and the government became deeply concerned.

The Catholic clergy in Quebec had good reason to worry. With increasing numbers of English coming into Canada, they foresaw the possibility that the French church might become a small island in a vast North American Protestant sea. To preserve the size and influence of the church they placed their hopes on two means: commitment to *La Survivance* and *la revanche de berceau*, or "revenge of the cradle" — a continued high French birth rate.[14] Emigration threatened both these methods. The French numerical superiority dissipated as the *Québécois* left Canada, and, without *habitants* on ancestral lands, the sacred unity of the family and traditional social order broke down. Assimilation into an English-speaking Protestant Canada would surely follow. Tirelessly, the clergy preached about the evils attendant upon leaving family and parish, accusing those who had left of seeking earthly pleasure and luxuries while warning the rest of the corrupting influence of the republican, Protestant country to the south.[15]

They also took a more constructive approach to the problem. Finally realizing that existing *seigneuries* were hopelessly over-crowded, Bishop Ignace Bourget of Montreal decided to look for other lands on which to create rural settlements. Together with the Bishop of Quebec, he established the Association for Colonizing the Eastern Townships in 1848 and petitioned the governor Lord Elgin for a special land grant in this traditionally English preserve on which landless French Canadians could settle. In response, the governor opened up land in two of the townships for this purpose.[16] This small effort to keep the *habitants* on Quebec farms did not divert more than a trickle of settlers away from the main channel running off the *seigneuries* to the United States. Several later attempts at colonization jointly sponsored by Church and government would attract more interest, but, in the main, the flow of [the] landless continued southward.[17]

The government also took steps to help keep the *Québécois* at home and on the farm. Government agents went into rural parishes to teach good agricultural practices. Agronomists wrote articles, published newspapers and established agricultural societies in order to inform farmers of new, more efficient methods of production. Fairs and contests offered rewards to farmers with high yields or superior stock breeds.[18] . . .

In 1849 the government of Canada was so alarmed at the outward migration of French Canadians that the Legislative Assembly appointed a select committee to "inquire into the Causes and Importance of the Emigration which takes place Annually from Lower Canada to the United States" and to ascertain "the best means to prevent that emigration for the future."[19] . . .

. . . It was clear from their research that emigration crossed class lines and that economic problems permeated the whole French

Canadian community. According to Committee findings, the rural parishes suffered not only the endemic problems of overpopulation, soil depletion and limited access to land but such added afflictions as crop destruction by the wheat fly and other diseases. The Committee also mentioned the specific problems of city workers, noting that the decline of the lumber industry in Montreal and of shipbuilding in Quebec sent many young men and their families in search of similar work in the United States. Meanwhile, young professionals found their fields glutted and preferred jobs open to sons of the elite while business positions were largely the preserve of the English.[20]

The report also made suggestions to help alleviate emigration. For those forced off *seigneuries*, the Committee proposed the reduction of costs of Crown lands and the easing of credit terms for their purchase. In addition, they suggested the government should build good roads to these new lands to enable farmers to get their produce to markets more easily and should continue to encourage the teaching of better agricultural methods. Finally, to employ those who had already moved from country to city, the Committee urged an increase in public works projects, the establishment of more manufacturing in Quebec, and the encouragement of theme industries with protective tariffs.[21]

Each of the suggestions made by the Select Committee eventually became policy in Canada but none soon enough to curb the out-migration of *Québécois* to the United States. Less than ten years later, in 1857, the Legislative Assembly again felt it necessary to select a special committee to examine the causes of emigration. That committee came up with similar conclusions and similar suggestions to alleviate the situation.[22] Still the migration continued, and after the American Civil War, when the United States was more fully industrialized, the steady flow became a torrent. The disequilibrium between over-populated rural Quebec and labor-hungry America in the last third of the nineteenth century led to the arrival of over 500,000 *Québécois* after 1870.[23]

Most of these post-war French Canadian immigrants came off Quebec farms to work in the shoe factories and textile mills of central and southern New England.[24] Many of the immigrants who came before the Civil War, however, arrived before the factories of New England were hiring large numbers of immigrant operatives. Their choice of home and occupation was different from those who came later, and their reasons for coming to America varied. Even their historical memory was different, for many of the earlier *émigrés* had experienced the Rebellions and the struggle to protect their French culture.[25] . . . According to Mason Wade, there was one group of pre-war immigrants who had formed a sizable and distinct French Canadian community by the 1850s. These were the Quebec immigrants who lived in and around Burlington, Vermont.[26] . . .

In the first five years of the 1860s the Burlington area witnessed the personal tragedies, the dislocations, and the economic expansion of wartime. The Civil War drained off young men in record numbers; some died on battlefields and in army hospitals, while others remained in the new territories they had visited. According to one estimate, less than half the thirty-four thousand Vermonters who left the state in the course of the war ever returned.[27] Those who did, however, benefited from the wartime industrial expansion, employment, and rising wages. During the course of the war, as demand for lumber and wood products increased and new tariff restrictions protected local manufacturing from foreign competition, the Burlington area thrived.

The textile industry in the Burlington area also weathered the transition to a peacetime economy. The cessation of war and the gradual resumption of domestic cotton shipments sustained the local cotton mill until, by 1870, it had expanded its work force to 108 operatives and its annual production to a value of $92,410.[28] Even the Burlington Woolen Mill in Winooski Falls, which had been the most dependent on Union army commissions, continued to thrive after the war. Demand for police and railroad employee uniforms supplanted army orders, and the woolen mill began producing "their specialty of indigo blue goods" to fill that demand.[29] By the 1880s the factory also manufactured "broadcloths, moscows, fancy suitings, ladies' dress goods and cloakings."[30]

The total immigration during the war years was insignificant, however, when compared to the flood of French Canadians that poured southward into the United States in the second half of the decade. It is impossible to know just how many *Québécois* arrived during these years, but, according to Mason Wade's research, 101,020 Canadians migrated to the United States between 1865 and 1869 of which "a very large part came from Quebec."[31]

Yolande Lavoie, in her study of French Canadian emigration, has estimated that, in New England alone, the Canadian-born population more than doubled between 1860 and 1870, reaching a total of 159,445.[32] These are the bare statistics of a phenomenon that Robert Rumilly has labeled *la grande émigration*.[33] Alexandre Belisle, in his *Histoire de la Presse Franco-Américaine,* described the physical reality behind those statistics:

> In the last week of April, 1869, trains coming from Canada and passing through St. Albans [Vermont] carried 2,300 French Canadian émigrés. Americans would come to Canada to hire employees and on May 3rd one train carried six hundred of them in cars locked, apparently to avoid confusion and make any desertion impossible.[34]

These *Québécois* left their farms, villages, and parishes for the same general reasons that had impelled earlier *émigrés* to leave - overpopulation, low agricultural output, and inadequate employment opportunities in French Canada. In 1866, the struggling Quebec economy suffered an additional blow, which acted as further inducement to the poor *habitant* to emigrate. The American government abrogated the Reciprocity Treaty with Canada in order to protect its domestic agriculture. The Quebec farmers, never able to compete successfully with American and Ontarian growers, now faced tariffs on produce sold to the United States, a burden that forced more of them either to subsistence farming or off their land. Meanwhile, the New England cotton industry, forced to reduce production when the Civil War interrupted shipment of cotton from the South, resumed its growth. The depletion of the Yankee work

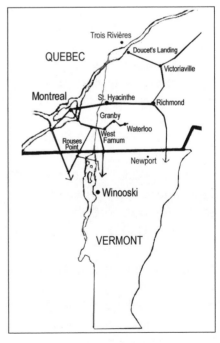

Canadian-Vermont Railroad Connections c.1865.
*(Source: Railways of Southern Quebec, Vol. 1)*

force from war and westward migration meant industrial jobs for all immigrants who sought them.[35]

Many of these poor French Canadian farmers and their families did not have to seek out factory positions; agents from the larger companies in such textile centers as Lowell and Lawrence, Massachusetts, and Manchester, New Hampshire, visited rural Quebec parishes and aggressively recruited them. With glowing reports of steady wages and extensive job opportunities they lured whole families, sometimes entire parishes, to their towns and mills. To both corporate owners and hungry French Canadian families the arrangement seemed ideal. The *émigrés* found work for several members of their large families while the employers gained an accessible, loyal, and uncomplaining work force.[36] Disrupted lives, crowded trains, arrival in an unfamiliar urban world, and the long, tedious hours of factory labor were harsh realities, but the prospect of weekly wages for several family members was preferable to the uncertainties, sometimes hopelessness, of farming in Quebec. . .

No agents from Burlington-area businesses traveled to Canada to recruit employees, however. For them recruitment was not necessary. The region was close to Canada and directly on the train route to southern New England. Those whose money ran out, those who wanted to remain near the Quebec border, those with friends or relatives in the region, and some who simply tired of traveling found the Burlington area a convenient or a necessary place to stop. In T. D. Seymour Bassett's words, they were "stranded before they reached their destination - stranded on the Vermont bridge" and created an influx of laborers without the cost of solicitation.[37]

The population figures for 1860 and 1870 reveal the impact of *la grande émigration* on the region. The total combined population of Burlington and Colchester rose about seventy percent, from 10,754 to 18,305, and the area's French Canadian population rose 171 percent, from 2,392 to 6,484 residents. While in 1860 French Canadians constituted less than one-fourth of the region's population, in 1870, over one-third of the area's residents were Quebec immigrants or their dependents. Furthermore, as had been the case in 1860, the French Canadians in 1870 represented a largely new group of settlers; only one hundred nine of the 1,039 families living in the region had been there ten years earlier.

Both the growth and the changing composition of the French Canadian population during the 1860s were dramatic in scope but were not new phenomena. Instead, they represented an acceleration of trends clearly established in the previous decade. A similar pattern

French Canadians from Missisquoi County, Quebec, in Winooski Mills, c.1895. *(By Irving C. Kennedy, courtesy of Vermont Historical Society)*

of change appeared in the employment choices of French Canadian workers. There was a continuous decline in the occupational status of the region's French Canadians from 1850 to 1870.

The percentage of Quebec immigrants in white collar and skilled labor positions, which at mid-century totaled 43.3 percent of the French Canadian work force, had declined to only 23.9 percent in 1870, leaving three out of every four male workers in low-paying unskilled jobs. Just how grave a problem this decline was for the economic condition of the French Canadian community is evident from the wage differential between skilled and unskilled labor in 1870. While a carpenter received an average of $3.50 per day, the common laborer received only half that wage, or $1.75 per day. Meanwhile, by 1870 the cost of board alone had climbed over 230 percent.[38]

The only way out of the financial bind of low wages and high costs was to put more family members to work. In 1870, 273 sons and daughters of French Canadian families, aged fifteen through nineteen, worked outside the home; the majority worked in the same low-paying positions that dependents in 1860 had held, such as factory operative and day laborer. Moreover, by 1870, child labor had become so common in the United States that the census for that year included occupations for all children above age nine, and in Burlington and Colchester sixty children, aged ten through fourteen, also held outside employment. . .

Meanwhile, the size of the families of French Canadians continued to rise. The combination of growing family size and declining occupational status without a comparable rise in the percentage of working dependents suggests that in 1870 a large number of these Burlington-area families did not make enough money to keep out of debt. While in 1850 families with fewer children and a father employed as a craftsman could survive with only one wage earner, these larger families in 1870, headed by unskilled laborers, likely found even subsistence problematic unless several family members worked. Given this increasing need for extra income, it seems doubtful that families chose to keep their children at home but rather that there were not enough available jobs in the Burlington area to employ all who wanted to work.

In the course of the 1860s, while Burlington had focused its economic development around mercantile business and small industries, Winooski had become a typical New England mill town, dominated by a large, absentee-owned textile operation, the Burlington Woolen Mill Company. By 1870, Burlington could no longer hold onto most of the Quebec *émigrés* who passed through the city on their way to communities with more promise of employment for young sons and daughters as well as full-grown men. By contrast, Winooski with the woolen mill, offered ample unskilled jobs to many family members. Throughout much of the nineteenth century, a steady stream of new French Canadian immigrants came to Winooski and stayed.

Excerpts are reprinted here with permission of the author. The entire thesis is at Special Collections, University of Vermont Libraries.

*Betsy Beattie is the Canadian Studies librarian at the University of Maine's Folger Library. In addition to a library degree, she has a master's degree from the University of Vermont and a doctorate from the University of Maine, both in Canadian history. She has written articles on Canadian migration to the United States from Quebec and from the Maritime Provinces. Her forthcoming book is* Obligation and Opportunity: Single Maritime Women in Boston, 1870 to 1930.

# In the Shadow of the Factory: Worker Housing in Winooski
## *by Susan Ouellette*

Starting with the industrial ventures along the Winooski River in the 1830s, local business and manufacturing leaders struggled to house a sufficient labor force within the town. They were not alone in this concern nor were they the first. Two decades earlier the Boston Associates, the corporate entity that created a similar textile complex on the Merrimac River at Lowell, Massachusetts, faced the same issues. Their remedy, known as the Waltham System, identified a specific kind of labor force and developed a particular strategy to attract and keep those workers. In sum, the Waltham system drew on the population of young unmarried farm daughters who were supposedly less useful on the farms once textile production shifted from the home to the factories. Young women made ideal factory operatives[1] since they were potentially cheap, malleable as workers and relatively available. The incorporation of strictly supervised boarding houses into the Lowell factory system made Yankee fathers more likely to allow their daughters to go into the factories. This model became the ideal for other developing textile centers around New England.[2]

With the Lowell experience to draw on, Winooski's industrial leaders learned that housing was crucial to attract and keep a sizable population of productive workers. In addition, there was more than just numbers to consider. Adequate housing in Winooski concerned employers' needs as well as employee comforts. Mill-owned or subsidized housing also meant that mill managers could potentially shape employee behavior outside of the factory walls. Just as important, in times of labor unrest, control over housing was an important tool in employer/employee negotiations. Consequently, mill workers' housing was as important to the commercial success of Winooski as the complex of industrial buildings perched along the riverbank.

As early as 1835, the Burlington Woolen Company began the process of providing lodgings to its operatives in Winooski.[3] Two dwelling types, boarding houses and tenements, became primary investments – after machinery and factory buildings – for these antebellum industrial employers. Together with a small number of modest one-family homes, tenements and boarding houses encompassed the range of housing options available to Winooski mill operatives through the nineteenth and into the twentieth centuries.

Boarding houses, the centerpiece of the Waltham system, provided Winooski with appropriate lodgings for the first wave of mill operatives: unmarried farm girls. These young women, most between the ages of fourteen and twenty-five, came chiefly from surrounding rural villages to earn cash wages not available to them on the farms.[4] Nearly all would not have been able to come to work in the mill had there not been appropriate "bed and board" facilities. Nineteenth century Yankee daughters were not permitted to set up on their own; their parents required that they be supervised and disciplined as though they still lived at home.

Meant to be extensions of Yankee farm households, boarding houses were generally leased or sold to respectable citizens in the community.[5] In Winooski there were approximately seven boarding house establishments by 1850. Married couples operated three while the remaining five were operated by widows.[6] Most of these establishments tended to have female boarders with "mill worker" listed as their occupation. In the years between 1850 and 1910, boarding houses continued to operate in the town, though the ethnicity of the mill girl population shifted from primarily Yankee to a mix of Irish and French Canadian operatives by the first decade of the twentieth century.[7]

Another parallel between the Lowell boarding houses and those in Winooski was the attempt by the boarding house managers to

Young girls working in American Woolen Mills, Winooski, 1909. *(by Lewis Hine, courtesy of Robert Hull Fleming Museum, University of Vermont, gift of Daniel K. Mayers)*

supervise their charges in a carefully structured environment. Under the eyes of their supervisors in the mill during the day, the young women were also regulated during their non-working hours.[8] Just as the Boston Associates emphasized intellectual and cultural activities for their workers, the Burlington-Winooski leaders hosted many similar diversions. A perusal of the *Burlington Daily Free Press* between 1849 and 1870 reveals regular announcements of musical evenings, public lectures and religious speakers; many performers came to Vermont directly from their Massachusetts engagements.[9]

To the chagrin of the Winooski mill owners and managers, yet another similarity between the Lowell and Winooski "girls" seems to have existed: their resistance to management practices they deemed exploitative or unfair.[10] Life in the close quarters of the boarding house meant female operatives developed close bonds with each other that could translate into a unified resistance to employer expectations. The "spinners strike" of 1865 was one instance where this collective spirit manifested. In February of that year, spinners in the woolen factory decided to strike in protest against the mill management's decision to fire one of the operatives. The *Free Press* reported that approximately thirty mill workers walked off their station and tried to bring the whole factory out. The mill supervisor sent for the sheriff, who promptly arrested the women. In the end, two of the "leaders" were fined ten dollars each "for breach of the peace" and the rest were discharged. Not once did the *Free Press* mention that the strikers were women, though in an earlier article the paper noted that spinners, doffers and weavers were almost exclusively female in the Winooski factories.[11]

In other ways, the concentration and proximity of operatives to the mill building was a distinct advantage to mill managers. Workers living close to the factory were readily available for the six twelve-hour workdays beginning at dawn; shirking or suffering from "Saint Monday" disease right under the very windows of the factory was difficult if not impossible. In addition, operatives living in the shadow of the factory could be quickly mobilized. One incident in 1849 is illustrative. In the early months of 1849, the Burlington Mill Company management experienced some difficulty with stockholders who forced the factory operations to stop. In June, a temporary agreement was reached that allowed the managers to re-start operations. According to the *Free Press*:

> [O]peratives were called together at five o'clock this morning and
> when the fact was known that the Looms would be immediately set to
> work, the most unequivocal expressions of gratification greeted the
> announcement, and a 'rush' was made by the 'gals' to see which
> should first start the hum of productive industry in the old familiar
> walls.[12]

Not only were the Burlington Mill Company managers able to
get the workers back into the factory the same day, but they were
able to assemble them at a very early morning hour.

Boarding houses remained an important housing component of
the Winooski complex long after the mills abandoned the Waltham
system. By the mid-twentieth century, they still functioned as
housing for unmarried operatives, though often those operatives
were immigrants. Many of the French Canadian mill operatives
who worked in Winooski preferred to board rather than establish
more permanent living quarters since they viewed their stay as
temporary. Their main goal was to save the money they earned;

Mill housing, Winooski. Left to right: brick boarding house (partly cut off), c.1840; white wooden
boarding house, c.1865; two brick overseer's cottages in front of the Congregational Church.
*(Courtesy of Special Collections, University of Vermont Libraries)*

they imagined life here in the mills as a necessary interlude before returning home to Quebec.

Tenements seem to have been primarily established for married workers who could not afford to buy a modest home. In Winooski, tenements customarily housed two to three families and seem also to have quickly become ethnically segregated. From 1850 to 1910, the number of dwellings housing multiple families rose by nearly fifty percent, as did the immigrant population of the town. The census schedules from those years indicate that operatives who lived in multiple family dwellings were far more likely to be Irish or French Canadian immigrants.[13] Both groups began to arrive in substantial numbers at mid-century, the French Canadians responding to a rural land crisis in lower Quebec and the Irish with the construction of the railroad that connected Winooski with the rest of New England. According to one federal study done in the 1930s, most of these immigrants settled in the factory towns of Vermont, particularly near the textile centers.[14]

The last type of housing available to married factory operatives, especially French Canadian families who managed to set aside a small cash reserve, was a modest single family home. In the last quarter of the nineteenth century, Francis LeClair, a local French Canadian entrepreneur, began to construct modest housing specifically for the mill operatives in Winooski. In a career than spanned 1849 to 1889, LeClair built and marketed at least seventy-five homes, often holding the mortgages himself.[15]

Into the mid-twentieth century, housing remained an important issue for mill management and town leaders as well as for the workers themselves. Large boarding houses became less prominent, but boarding continued to be an important option. By 1910, single operatives were more likely to live in family homes sharing space with host families and one or two other boarders. The number of tenement apartments increased, perhaps reflecting the downward economic slide from the 1920s onward into the Great Depression. Single-family homes continued to be built, though on smaller houselots with less room for the gardens and sideyards of the late nineteenth century.

In the 1950s, the press for housing sharply decreased with the closing of the mills. Instead of families and single workers coming to Winooski, textile workers packed up and left. According to one historian, housing became very inexpensive as people migrated out of Winooski in search of work.[16] The homes that Francis LeClair so painstakingly built, the boarding houses that teemed with young people and the tenements bursting with young families were abandoned to people too old or too poor to leave.

In recent years, the mill buildings abandoned by the textile manufacturers have again become central to Winooski's economic development. The Champlain Mill has metamorphosed into shopping space, providing a modest number of jobs compared to its original capacity. Even more ironic is the transformation of other mill structures into moderate and high-end housing. Rather than creating a need for housing in Winooski, the old mills now fulfill that role.

Francis LeClair (1818-1889). *(From* Histoire de la Congrégation Canadienne *by J.-F. Audet, 1898)*

*Susan Ouellette, a specialist in Colonial American history at Saint Michael's College, earned her master's and doctorate degrees from the University of Massachusetts, and her bachelor's degree from SUNY Plattsburgh. She has sub-specialities in nineteenth century American social history and French Canada/Northeastern Native Peoples. She published "Divine Providence and Collective Endeavor: Sheep Production in Early Massachusetts" in* The New England Quarterly *in 1996, and has entries in* The American Heritage Encyclopedia of American History.

# The Star Bakery
## *Recollections of Frank Perrino*

My name is Frank Perrino. They call me Chichil. When I was about six years old I started working in the bakery because the owner of the bakery was my stepfather. I started wrapping bread. A guy come from Philadelphia as a salesman. And he'd say Frank how about timing you on wrapping bread. Course then the store just had a machine that would seal 'em but you have to wrap 'em. I did twenty-eight a minute. I got six cents a week, enough to go to the movies.

Then I started working in the pastry. We had the biggest line of pastry, French pastry and Italian pastry. Course my brother-in-law, Joe Mazza, was the head one. We used to make the Napoleons. We'd make 'em long and then we'd cut 'em in squares. But the trouble is, the ones that worked in the bakery, we ate all the profit. So my stepfather says I don't make no more he says because no profit. And that's the way we'd go.

The salesmen were the ones that taught you how to make different things and how to use a decorator. Like my brother-in-law, he didn't go to school very much but he learned a lot. They had this guy. His name was Earl Blanchard. Boy that guy was good. He could make flowers on your cake with the frosting and everything. French. Yup. Earl Blanchard.

Trono's Star Bakery. Left to right: Joseph Mazza, George Pepin, John Trono and Frank Perrino, c. late 1920s. *(Courtesy of Madeline and Frank Perrino)*

The salesmen would tell you if you run into problems to call certain place and a guy will come. They knew how to make any kind of pastry. My stepfather would say, "What have you got that I should be using, I got a lot of French people here." And the guy understood 'cuz the French people from Canada all came in. And they liked sweet stuff like pastry. [The salesmen] would give us recipes that they would make like Napoleons and moguls and jelly doughnuts and plain doughnuts and butter doughnuts.

Mogul is a sheet a cake. It's thin, maybe a quarter of an inch. Then they put the cream in there. It's a cream that they mixed with marshmallow and confectionery sugar and they put a little bit of honey and coloring in it. That's the way they made the inside filling. They'd roll 'em up, roll 'em up, roll 'em up and then they'd put a fudge frosting on top.

The best thing for a dessert is take one mogul and a pint of cream. That's what we'd have, that and the milk and oh it was beautiful, the pastry. Then we made the cherry tarts in a cup the way they make cupcakes. They put pineapple on the bottom and they put cherry filling on the top and they put whipped cream on top. You know the French people, I'm telling you, they used to eat it up.

They used to make gilets, the French call 'em gilet. They take 'em, they cut 'em and they roll 'em out. They put 'em in hot crisco and they fry 'em, then they turn 'em over, then they'd put honey on 'em or whatever, because they couldn't eat meat on Friday. So they had to have bread dough.

Friday and Saturday was the best day for bread dough. And some of them, you know, they were smart. There was one guy, he lived down on Fort Pick. This guy would come in, he'd say "Give me ten cents of bread dough. So he take it and he'd go home. He had the [dough] for a loaf of bread. He made for ten cents a nice loaf of bread instead of paying let's say fifteen-sixteen cents.

During the week we didn't make as much. So that [Friday] was a big day. And he'd [stepfather] always say "hurry up, hurry up." He'd stay in the back; he'd watch us; (knock knock) he'd rap on the table. "Chichil hurry up. Wait on them fast, you know the people don't wanna hang around, they don't want to stay in line." So the quicker you take care of the customer the next customer has his chance.

[When] a mother comes in with a child, my stepfather used to say, "You know, you gotta watch the business. You gotta give the little boy a little cookie. By doing that, when he grows up he's gonna come back here and he's gonna buy bread, he's gonna buy anything he wants. Who knows. His mother says, "Go to the store and buy a bread or something." He's gonna come down here. You know, he [stepfather] was smart, he had it all up here [in his head]. So the little boy come over so I did what he said.

The cookies went good. So we'd make a lot more cookies. I think it was twelve cents a dozen at that time. And [squares], I hate to say the price but they were five cents a square. They were big squares. Today you'd have to pay fifty cents for one. And we had the penny pies. We used to have tins. They would put a layer of pie crust. Then we put apricot, apple, raisin, there was five or six kinds. Oh and lemon they had. We put the filling inside, the pie crust on top. You wouldn't frost them, you'd just leave them like that because the taste was right there with the fillings.

We make our filling ourselves instead of buying it. The salesmen would come [with] all the ingredients like cream and marshmallow and all that. They had these fifty gallon barrels that the marshmallow came in. You could [have] so many barrels, what are you gonna do with'em. So then they'd sell 'em sometimes to the ones that are making wine. They use 'em cause they were big thick barrels.

We was the only place that used pure cream for their cream puffs. He was a milkman, but he had a store. His name was Mercure. We didn't want to keep extra so he'd [Mercure] send this kid up, get a quart of cream or a pint of cream, cause cream, you didn't want to keep too much on hand. Who had a Frigadaire them days there.

We made wedding cakes. My God. We made our wedding cake. Madeline [Frank's wife] adds: "Oh God, fruitcakes." About five or six layers. We had to take it, my dad had a Pierce Arrow car and in them days Pierce Arrow, by God that was the biggest car. So we took the cake to White River [where they were married]. We had to sit in the back seat and we put the wedding cake on a pail and we guided it, because we didn't want it to tip over. And of course my brother-in-law came so he brought the stuff that he needed to fix it if it did something. [He did have to fix it] because it would shake because the roads weren't the same as today. They were all a, how'd you call the roads, sand roads, gravel stuff like that. Oh I tell you.

We used to put in a lot of hours in there. We had to work six days a week. You had Saturday off, but you had to come in Sunday. See the bread, when they make the doughnuts and the bread, we started on Sunday. But we didn't get no time and a half from them. My stepfather started at four o'clock in the morning, every morning. But at noon he would come upstairs, have his dinner and then he'd go lay down for two, three hours. That was a tradition that he'd do. He brought it [from Italy]. He'd come back downstairs and got prepared to make some more stuff or got ideas what to make for the next day. You didn't sell all this stuff. He'd have a list like he gotta make some cookies, jelly rolls, doughnuts.

Plus we had a camp in South Hero. He'd take the boys, my brothers and myself. He had an orchard, two orchards. He had business on his mind. He had apple trees, pear trees and all that stuff up there. Those apples, he had different kinds that he would use in the bakery.

We used to have boarders then. I had to sleep with the boarder who used to leave me five cents under the pillow each day. Yeah, we had to go to school. I got out a school early [to work at the bakery]. I only went to the sixth grade I think. Oh them days there, money was scarce and when we got paid, whatever we got we gave it to our mother. And my mother would say, "No Chichil, you gotta keep some." No, you know, you was compelled to give the money to them [parents]. You know for, to take care of us.

When the mill closed the bakery closed 'cuz there was no business.

*Frank Perrino grew up on River Street in Winooski. His father, John Perrino, worked at the mill. Later, when his mother married John Trono, they moved to an apartment above the bakery, across from the Woolen Mill. He started work at the bakery. When he was old enough, he worked third shift at the mill, carding and spinning, and weekends at the bakery, ten or twelve hours a day. After the mills closed, he worked in shipping and stocking at General Electric.*

# SECTION FOUR

# Many Languages, Many Cultures

# French Winooski, *le p'tit Canada*
## *by Kim Chase*

Of all the immigrant groups in Winooski, the French Canadians were the only ones to come into this country by land. They lived peacefully with Poles, Italians and Irish, but had little need to interact with any but their own people. When my mother was growing up in Winooski in the twenties and thirties, it could be said that everyone French in town was delivered by a Thabault and buried by a LaVigne, three generations of doctors and undertakers. Eli LaVigne, son of Arthur, provided Winooski with its first ambulance service.

In between the Thabaults and the LaVignes, there was someone in French Winooski to provide everything anyone needed. The Richards owned the only farm within city limits; Eugene Richard, brother of the farmer, ran the furniture factory. Hormidas J. Mercure operated the dairy. François Niquette was a grocer; his son Russell was a lawyer. Monsieur Frégeau was the cobbler, Origène Bergeron the blacksmith, Emilien Brault the barber

George Thabault, M.D., c. 1910.
*(Courtesy of Sr. Marion Chaloux, Fanny Allen Hospital)*

and Monsieur Huard the photographer. All three pharmacists in town were French: Dufresne, Marcotte and Richard. The mayor was Armand Rathé. The French had the police department squared away with Officers St-Amour, Cinq-Mars and Chief Charlie Barber (originally Baboeuf or Babeu). Monsieur Gélineau took care of everyone's insurance.

---

**MARCOTTE BROS., DRUGGISTS,**

Sell and Guarantee WHITE PINE AND TAR COUGH SYRUP at 25 cents per bottle. Money Refunded if it fails to Give Satisfaction.

(From *1899 Winooski, Vt*)

Many of the French in Winooski contributed services from their homes in addition to holding full-time jobs and raising astonishingly large families. My great-grandfather, Séverin Beaudoin was a raconteur who presided over frequent *soirées* at his home. My great-grandmother, Adéline Beaudoin, called *la mère Beaudoin* in town, was a midwife and my grandmother, Amanda Beaudoin Bouffard, was one of many professional seamstresses. My grandfather, Alphonse Bouffard, worked most of his life in the drawing room at the Mill; he was also a finish carpenter like his father, and was often called upon to build cabinets and staircases.

French rum-runners provided crime and excitement during Prohibition. Their operation required two vehicles. A car without contraband would lead the police on a high speed chase, crossing the border in Highgate and eventually tearing through Winooski on Main Street. Meanwhile, the car with all the goods would cross the border through a farmer's field or on a remote country lane at a law-abiding speed. When the police caught up with the decoy, all they could issue was a speeding ticket. Should the rum-runners fail, there was always Madame LaFrance who made bootleg liquor right in town.

Saint Francis Xavier Church, Winooski. *(by Pascal Roche)*

French Winooski's spiritual needs were met by Father Lacouture, the parish priest at Saint Francis Xavier, and the good sisters of Providence at *Couvent St. Louis*, the French elementary school. *Les enfants de Marie* was run by local spinsters who took it upon themselves to attend to the moral edification of adolescent girls who generally joined the organization on leaving the *Couvent* and going on to high school. Like other *p'tits Canadas* throughout New England, Winooski had its branches of *L'Union Saint-Jean-Baptiste* and *Les dames de Sainte-Anne*, cultural societies associated with the French Catholic church. The Union of St. John the Baptist was and continues to be a business society providing its members with insurance policies and functioning as a kind of French old boys' network. The Sodality of Ladies of St. Anne is a

Saint Francis Xavier Church during renovations, c. 1941. *(Courtesy of Kim Chase)*

spiritual society for parish women who gather on a regular basis for their spiritual edification.

Family vacations in mill town Winooski meant only one thing to the French: visiting relatives who lived away. Sometimes folks made excursions elsewhere in New England where another branch of the family had relocated, but more typically they went to Canada, always to visit family. Taking a trip which did not involve visiting relatives was as likely as taking a trip to the moon.

Each summer, some contingent of my mother's extended family went to Québec to visit her great uncle Prosper LaRoche, a farmer in La Patrie, Quebec. They packed as many people from Winooski as possible into two cars, switching places in St. Johnsbury where they stopped for a picnic. They always arrived late at night and Prosper's wife, Délina, (*tante* Dina to the kids), would be waiting with mountains of ham sandwiches and pitcher after pitcher of fresh, cold milk.

All the Canadians got up when the visitors arrived, including the children who had to make space for the American cousins. They threw down extra feather beds or corn husk mattresses, sometimes lining the smaller kids up across the bed to fit them all on. Délina had made the mattresses herself and spun her own wool from which she wove blankets, knitted hats, sweaters, mittens and afghans. She quilted *couvre-pieds* (quilts), made from sewing scraps, and white rag rugs called *catalognes*. She made her own soap from lye and suet, cutting great bars of yellow for laundry and heavy cleaning, and smaller, white bars for toilet soap. She put up almost all the food her family would need for the winter and also helped to care for the horses, sheep, pigs and chickens.

The LaRoches rose at four o'clock to do morning chores while tante Délina cooked breakfast. All the children helped; the youngest could pick berries while the older kids milked the cows. On my mother's last visit, her cousins picked fourteen quarts of strawberries before breakfast. They hulled them right in the field so *tante* Dina had only to wash them before setting a bowlful on the table. They ate them with sugar and fresh, golden cream plus a thick slice of Délina's homemade bread and butter. For the Americans, this was a heavenly breakfast but for the Canadian farmers, it was only a beginning. Typically, their morning meal consisted of fried salt pork, potatoes and gravy, roast pork or ham, eggs, cheese, great pitchers of cream and *ma tante's* French bread toasted on the top of the cast iron stove. Délina said Americans didn't know how to eat.

After breakfast, the farmers let the visitors help with chores, although my mother always suspected they were really in the way. The kids helped feed the chickens and sheep while the men helped out in the fields and in the barn.

Lunch was another big meal, but supper, *le souper*, was just that, a rich soup which Délina had simmering all day on the stove, plus a few more loaves of her homemade bread. This simple meal was a favorite among the American cousins, to the amusement of the Canadians.

"You poor, underfed Americans!" they laughed.

Sometimes after supper, Prosper and Délina hung glass and metal lanterns all around the kitchen and pushed the long table back against the wall to make space for a quadrille. They invited neighbors, usually related in one way or another, and brought in extra chairs to form a circle around the big room. There was a fiddler in every *rang*, or every country road, and everyone else tapped feet during the *soirée*.

One night, Prosper invited some *bons gars Cana'iens,* good Canadian boys, to the quadrille. They were lumberjacks, huge men with bushy beards, each over six feet tall in red shirts and suspenders. They laughed loudly and reeked of wood smoke, but they were an honest, friendly bunch. After they left, Prosper asked my mother what she thought of his *bûcherons;* although she did not

Family of Sévérin Beaudoin and Adéline (Laroche) Beaudoin, Winooski, Vermont, c.1915. Left to right, seated: Amanda (Bouffard), Sévérin, Ruth, Arthur, Adéline, Sévérin Jr. Standing: Estelle (Dupont) Roméo, Florence, Rodolphe, Célina (Gauthier), Wilfrid, Éva (Parizo), Napoléon, Laura, Gaudias. Missing: Azarias who died in Québec, Canada and Théodore, born in Winooski, who died twelve days after birth. *(Courtesy of Kim Chase)*

want to insult him, she let him know they were not to her liking.

"Well, I'll tell you something," Prosper declared, "Better to marry a good red-blooded Canadian than some *touche-minette*, pale-faced American!" My mother was too well acquainted with French Canadian pride to argue. She knew the Canadians considered the American cousins soft and spoiled.

Likewise, the French in Winooski questioned the morality of relatives who had relocated to Lowell, Massachusetts or to some of the other big mill towns. And just as my mother's family went to Canada to visit relatives, family from Lowell often came to Winooski for vacations. It was a tradition to arrive unannounced to see how long they could go unrecognized. Once, when my mother was young, a stranger at the door asked for my grandmother Amanda by name. My mother fetched her and when she appeared, the stranger asked in French if she could direct him to the house of Sévérin Beaudoin.

"Why, yes," my grandmother said. "My father and brother both answer to that name." At that, the stranger removed his hat and

Amanda yelled "Hilaire!" In a moment, she was in his arms. Shocked at the sight of a strange man kissing her mother, my mother ran to get her father. But Alphonse's reaction was no better. "Hilaire!" he cried and the two men began thumping each other's backs for all they were worth. He was a cousin and Alphonse's childhood friend before his family had moved to Lowell.

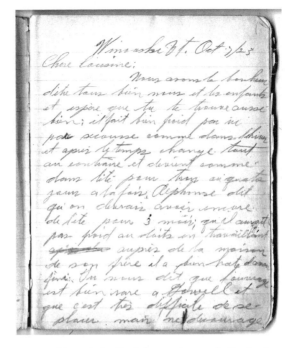

A page of Amanda Bouffard's letter to her cousin, October 7, 1923. *(Courtesy of Kim Chase)*

I have a letter my grandmother Amanda sent to a girl cousin who had left Winooski to work in Lowell. Amanda must have dictated it to my grandfather for it is in his hand and dated 1923, before she had taught herself to read and write. She comments on job opportunities:

> *"On dit l'ouvrage est bien rare à Lowell et que c'est très difficile de se placer mais ne décourage toi pas parce que dans le temps qu'on attend le moins c'est dans ce temps-là qu'on se place; dans tous les cas si tu ne te places pas à Lowell, tu penseras à Winooski; des fois on a de la chance dans une place qu'on n'aurait pas dans un autre. Il y a bien de l'ouvrage à Winooski jusqu'à présent."*

> "We hear there's not much work in Lowell and that it's difficult to get a job but don't be discouraged because you could find work when you least expect it. In any case, if you don't find work in Lowell, think of Winooski; sometimes you find luck in one place after being unlucky in another. Right now there's a lot of work in Winooski."

The encouraging tone of the letter changes to gentle disapproval when Amanda addresses the question of the opposite sex. Folks in French Winooski considered cities like Lowell worldly places full of temptations and unsuitable characters:

> *"Je suis bien fière que tu as rencontré plusieurs garçons et que tu as eu bien du plaisir; et tu me demandes ce que je ferais si j'étais à ta place quand un garçon te demande pour t'embrasser; et bien moi je le refuserais toujours combien même que c'est la façon à Lowell parce que si un garçon est respectable et pense à faire un avenir de bonheur en ménage il est capable d'attendre après qu'il est marié, ou au moins après son engagement et quand tu refuses d'embrasser un garçon s'il est smatte il pensera bien plus de toi; c'est la manière d'un garçon de connaître une fille. Quand un garçon baise une fille, il se vente de toutes ces choses qui c'est passé entre les deux."*

> "I'm proud that you've met several boys and that you've had a lot of fun. You ask what I would do if I were you when a boy asks to kiss you. Me, I would always refuse him even if they do that sort of thing in Lowell because if a boy is respectable and thinks about having a happy home in the future, he can wait until after he's married or at least until he's engaged and when you refuse to kiss a boy, if he's smart he will think even more of you. That's how a boy gets to know a girl. When a boy kisses a girl, he brags about what went on between the two of them."

My mother was born in the house her father and grandfather built on the corner of Burling Street, the same house we visited every summer when I was a child in the 1960s. Carrying on the family tradition, our two-week annual vacation was always spent with family. Although everyone tried to accommodate anglophone relatives, most conversations were in French.

The world has changed greatly since then, Winooski included. Yet, to this day, I would venture to say that there are still folks in French Winooski who can carry on without speaking a word of English.

*Kim Chase is a second-generation bilingual Franco-American.*
*A French teacher and free-lance writer, she has published several*
*articles and short stories on Franco-American culture and educa-*

*tional issues. Her family comes from Winooski. Her mother worked for a short time in the mill. This essay recounts experiences of the Beaudoin-Bouffard family in Winooski and Quebec.*

# The Winooski Irish
*by Vincent Feeney*

Next to the French Canadians, the Irish were the largest ethnic group in nineteenth century Winooski. In fact, in the 1840s and 1850s there were almost as many Irish as there were French Canadians living in the village. Only when Irish emigration to America slowed down in the latter half of the nineteenth century did the French-Canadian population of Winooski come to dwarf that of the sons and daughters of the Emerald Isle.

Jobs attracted the Irish to Winooski. In the 1840s, just as Ireland was experiencing its worst famine in history – the potato crop failed in 1845, 1846 and 1848 – Vermont was entering the industrial age. As unskilled workers, Irishmen crisscrossed New England looking for work, and Winooski had plenty. Textile mills, sawmills, railroad works and foundries employed hundreds. Winooski was a magnet for men who had little to offer beyond their strong backs and a willingness to work hard.

Unlike the Irish who settled in southern New England and New York, however, most of the Irish who came to reside in Winooski had arrived in the New World via the ports of Quebec City and Montreal. Not wanting to reside in the British Empire, they either walked to Vermont, or found passage on one of the steamships moving passengers from St. Jean in Quebec to ports on Lake Champlain. In this way, by the end of the 1840s, both Burlington and Winooski had large Irish populations.

How big was the Irish presence in Winooski in the mid-nineteenth century? It is difficult to get an accurate figure for two reasons: first, the figures in early census reports are only for Colchester Town, as Winooski was not yet a separate jurisdiction; second, many people whose nativity was given as Canada – and one might assume were French Canadians – were in fact the children of Irish immigrants. There was, for example, a family by the name of Grinen living in Winooski in the 1850s. The mother and father, Michael and Nancy, were born in Ireland, but their three children were born in Canada. Obviously the family had spent some time living in Canada before entering the United States. If one tabulated ethnicity from nativity alone, one would get a distorted view of the population.

The 1850 census for Colchester showed 218 Irish-born and 342

Lafayette Hose Company, Winooski, 1911. *(Courtesy of the Winooski Historical Society)*

Canadian-born people residing in Colchester. Almost all of these immigrants would have been found in Winooski, for that's where the jobs were. Given our caveat about the Canadian figures, it is probably safe to say that in 1850, French Canadians constituted only a slight majority of Winooski's ethnic makeup. In later years this would change, as emigration from Canada increased while that from Ireland declined.

That same 1850 census tells us something about the kinds of work engaged in by the Irish. Six Irishmen described themselves as "mill" laborers, while a significant number said they worked on the railroad. However, most simply put "laborer" under job description, suggesting that they did not identify with any one industry, but moved from job to job as the market demanded; one month they might be working in the woolen mill, and another month putting out lumber at the sawmill.

Significantly, occupations were not listed for women, suggesting either that the census takers discounted their work, or that Irishwomen at this early date in Winooski had not yet entered the work force outside the home. However, one should note that the Harding brothers who owned the mills, and who lived at the Mansion House on the corner of Main and Mansion streets, employed Irish girls as domestic servants in the 1850s.

By 1890 the picture had changed. The census for that year lists the majority of Irish Americans living in Winooski as working for the woolen mills. Most were weavers – both men and women – but men could also be found running the carding machines, working in the sorting rooms, and as cloth examiners (perchers or burlers). A significant number described themselves as "mill laborer," suggesting that they had no particular function, but moved from assignment to assignment within the mill.

As time passed and immigrants became permanent residents, a distinctive Irish community formed in Winooski. The heart of this community was the South Ward – the area south of the railroad tracks and closest to the mills – particularly West Allen Street, which contained so many Irish that it was popularly known as Cork Alley. The McGraths, Sullivans, Hallorans, Hennesseys, Bourkes, Learys, Collins and others lived along this street in the 1890s.

By the turn of the century the Winooski Irish had established their own organizations and institutions. Most important was their church. When the French-speaking people built St. Francis Xavier in 1870, the Irish community established St. Stephens Parish in 1871. While it catered to all Winooski's English-speaking Catholics, St. Stephens was always known as the "Irish" Church.

Two Winooski institutions had a surprising Irish orientation: the fire department and the public schools. Because Winooski's lone parochial school, St. Louis Convent, conducted classes in French, Irish Catholics tended to send their children to the public schools. Moreover, bright young Irish women who aspired to make something of themselves often became teachers. By 1900 Winooski's public schools were staffed principally by Irishwomen with names like Lonergan, Walsh, Welch, Farrell, Geary and Mulqueen.

Something similar happened in Winooski's fire department, which, by the 1880s and 1890s, consisted of two volunteer companies, the Winooski Steamer Company and the Lafayette Hose Company. In those days fire departments not only served a protective function but were like clubs; they elected officers, put on entertainments and had athletic teams. Most importantly, the fire departments represented specific classes within a community. The Steamer Company, for example, was made up of the Republican business interests in town, the old Yankees if you will. The Lafayette Hose Company despite its French name was Irish working class, Winooski's exclusive Irish club. In 1901, its list of officers read like an Irish telephone directory: Fitzgerald, O'Sullivan, Burke, Buckley, Hennessey, Finnegan and O'Dea.

Much has been written about the tensions between the Irish and their fellow Catholics in the French Canadian community, and much of it is true. The two did look at each other with some suspicion – how else to explain the existence of separate French and Irish churches in Winooski and other New England towns. There is the story told to me by a native of Winooski of a relative whose French-speaking mother told her to exchange her Irish boyfriend for a French boy who was then dating an Irish girl. This, the mother thought, would make everyone happy. Yet with all these stories about Irish-French tensions, many Winooski families today are products of French-Irish unions.

Perhaps the story of the O'Brien family best illustrates the Irish experience in Winooski. Edward and Ellen O'Brien from County Roscommon immigrated to the United States in 1890, and settled in Winooski where Edward got a job as a watchman at the woolen mill. One of their sons, John, born in 1892, went to work as an office boy in the mill at age fourteen. There he later met and married Yvonne Provost, a young French-Canadian mill worker in Winooski. Love must have conquered all for when they met neither could speak the other's language.

Due to his intelligence and hard work, O'Brien went from promotion to promotion. In 1931, he was named general superintendent, the number two position in the mills, and in 1948, he rose to the top position, general manager. Of John and Yvonne's three boys, two became doctors and one a lawyer. Through work afforded them in Winooski, countless Irish families, like the O'Briens, went from penniless immigrants to American success stories.

*Vincent Feeney is an adjunct professor of Irish history at the University of Vermont and a real estate broker. Currently, he is president of the Chittenden County Historical Society, writes a column entitled "Out of our Past" for the Winooski Eagle, and is working on a history of Winooski.*

**Addendum:**
The O'Briens of Chittenden County:
Proud, prominent, plentiful and a little confusing.
It's not easy, lad, said Kevin Kilcoyne, the wisest of them all. Well,

the O'Briens of Chittenden County are senators and salesmen, lawyers and dancers, physicians and cattlemen, judges and nurses. And they are also teachers and real estate dealers, postal workers, printers, hairdressers, engineers and insurance men. It's because they are so prominent and plentiful that others are confused. Sometimes there are even Irish who are uncertain. It's hard enough that they have the same last name. But there are some with

*(Courtesy of Helene O'Brien)*

the same first names which necessarily make middle initials the name of the game – and sometimes even they are the same. Remember this above all, Kevin Kilcoyne continued, few of the O'Brien families are related.

Bear in mind, of course, that Dr. Robert E. O'Brien of Winooski is not related to any of the South Burlington O'Briens, nor to Robert A. O'Brien of Shelburne. But he is the son of Rep. John E. O'Brien [who is also general manager of American Woolen in Winooski] and the brother of Probate Judge J. William O'Brien.

Kevin Kilcoyne closed his notebook and called for another round.

*Excerpts from writings by Joe Heaney, courtesy of Dr. Robert E. O'Brien.*

# Italians in Winooski
## *Recollections of Madeline Perrino*

My name is Madeline Perrino. I've been living in Winooski for fifty-nine years. My mother, Jennie (Genoeffa) Izzo came from the village of Rotondi and my father, Patsy (Pasquale) Gallo came from Paolisi. They lived about one mile from one another, but they never met when they were in Italy. They came to Ellis Island. They came for jobs.

My father came first and lived in White River Junction, Vermont. When my mother arrived at Ellis Island, she went to White River where she stayed with her sister Giovanina. That's where she met my father. They married there and raised four daughters, Rose (Rosa), Madeline (Maddelena), Lena (Pasqualina), Josephine (Geppine) and one son, Ralph (Raffaele).

X locates Paolisi and Rotondi, the small mountain villages where Madeline Perrino's parents grew up.

Many of the Italians went to work in Barre on account of the quarries. In White River it was the railroads. They came [to Winooski] for the woolen mills or because someone in their family or someone [else] had come from their part of Italy. They had a padrone who would find them a job and place to live. And because the first ones found there was work here, more would come whenever they had the money. That's how my mother came over. Her sister came to America first, then she wrote my mother to come. White River, that's where I was born.

My dad worked very hard on the railroad. Sometimes he would be gone for four or five days at a time, mostly in the wintertime. Many times he worked sixteen to twenty-four hours straight. They would take the caboose to clear the snow and check the railroad tracks. They slept and ate on the caboose. They had to make sure the tracks were open for the trains that were coming through because White River Junction was a big railroad center, oh it was so enormous that [trains] came from all over.

[People were] very, very poor in Italy. I remember my mother sending bags of clothing there. The only thing you could put 'em in was those soft flour bags that had to be washed and washed, and then sew them at the top. She used to send oh so many of those [to Italy] because they didn't have anything. But now they have nothing to worry about. They have their own homes and cars and their homes are beautiful. I've been there.

We visited the little villages where my mother and father came from and saw the places where my mother used to work in Italy. My mother used to climb the mountain. She used to say it was straight up. She used to go out and collect twigs for the fireplace and place them on her head to walk down the mountain. She'd pick chestnuts, place them in a large basket which she placed on her head. I think that's why my mother walked so straight. Most of those Italian women walked so straight. My grandmother used to do the same thing. They had a special place where they could stop and have a lunch, cheese and bread. The women worked hard in Italy. The men would walk to places looking for work and return home when they could.

[My mother] told us a lot of things about Italy, how they cele-brated their festival days, mostly to honor the saints and certain Holy Days. In her village it was for Maria SS. Della Stella; in another village it would be for Saint Anthony, etc. There are bands that play. People take part in singing Italian songs. Italian sweets are sold like biscotti, figs, torrone nuts, chestnuts and gelato (ice cream). At night they would have a concert.

I don't remember any festivals in Winooski. At Christmas time the families would get together. In our house we had everything Italian, all Italian food. My mother used to make her own bread, make her own pasta. My mother and father used to have a big garden and some vegetables in White River Junction. They didn't have much money, but they worked hard. And we all played sports together. We didn't have baseball bats or balls. We used to make our own with leftovers. My mother used to have rags and we used to make our own balls. We used a piece of wood for a bat.

In Winooski there were some [Italians] here, some there. But in White River Junction it was all Italians living on South Main

Street. They came from all over Italy. Most of them came from Calabria, Sicilia, Napoli, Bari, Salva, Foggia, Paolisi and Rotondi. I met one woman from Genoa. She came from Barre because she had lost her husband and she married an Italian from Winooski. She was a nice woman. There were a lot of nice Italians. In fact, I knew all of 'em cause we used to visit each other. And the funniest part of it was, while I was talking to all these Italians, I was learning how to speak Calabrese and Genoese. And I knew some Neopolitan. I also knew Sicilian. We spoke Italian at home all the time. I still speak Italian.

My husband's name is Frank Perrino, he's better known as Chichil. Everyone knows him in Winooski, cause everyone tells me, oh you're married to Chichil. He's lived in Winooski eighty-five years, that's how old he is. His family was here already. His father came first, then his mother came. They came from Sava, on the Adriatic Sea.

I met Chichil when I was going to the University of Vermont. I met him on Church Street. He was with his friend Joe Zelonis. He's Polish. They were walking up Church Street and we happened to meet 'em. So my friend says oh I want you to meet one of our friends. So they introduced me, this is Madeline Perrino, uh Madeline Gallo, and so, oh I said, it's nice to meet you. Then they left; we kept on walking. So I didn't think anything about it. He told me after we got married, you know what I said after I met you? I wouldn't marry her, she wears glasses. We were married and we've been married for fifty-nine happy years.

When I went to college, the tuition was $125. I didn't live in the dorm, couldn't afford it. But I did live in the co-op house. There were thirteen women there. The rent was twelve dollars a month. We would take turns to cook lunch and dinner so we had a little time off in between. That first year I worked all summer long to pay for my tuition. When I was in college I worked too. I was paid thirty-five cents an hour in the late 1930s. I worked in the YMCA enough just to pay for the twelve dollars for my room. My parents always told us you've got to go to school; you've got to have a good education.

In 1939, I went to White River where I taught elementary school one year. I married my husband in White River and I came to Winooski to live. Right after that I said I think I should go work in the mill. Because at that time women could not get work as teachers, there were mostly men teaching in Vermont. When the war broke out, the [women] teachers had plenty of work because the men left. Then the men came back. Some of them replaced [the women]. A lot of the [women] teachers left their jobs; they just retired.

I worked in the Chace Mill for six months; it was hard work. I was paid thirty-five cents an hour; my pay for the week was, I think, thirteen dollars, in late 1941. The wages were very low here. I saw a lot of older women lifting up these heavy, heavy spools of cotton, and I said to myself: Oh my God I don't know how they can do that. No man would help them. I can still see those Italian women. They did all that hard work with the spools.

Then I went to the Woolen mill where I worked in the sewing department. When I went in the front door which is now the entrance to the Woolen Mill apartments, I used to hold my nose, because there was such a stink. They used to wash the wool there, and you know how wool smells. I used to walk through there fast. We used to go through the weave room, the clickety clack, clickety clack all the time. I didn't like that. But when we got to the sewing department it was quiet. We could talk where we were, because we were so far away from the looms. We would sew the army and navy blankets that had mispics which was if there was anything wrong like missing threads, we'd have to sew that in. Only two of us spoke English. The rest of them spoke French. I met a very good friend, Doris Hebert that was working next to me. We couldn't speak French. We didn't know what they were talking about. So we finally says well we'll talk English all we can, so we did. Then one day we said why don't we make up something and jibber jabber. So we jibbered and jabbered for about half a minute and then we started to laugh so we didn't try it any more.

After I worked in the sewing department, I folded blankets. The war had ended, but they were still making army and navy blankets. We used to fold hundreds and hundreds of those every day. We had to pull down these heavy, heavy rolls of material. Just yank 'em down all the time. I'd have to raise my arms and then we would fold [the blankets] while they were in the air. I really think that's what started my trouble now because I have arthritis. When we worked in the sewing department, we sat down, but in the blanket department we stood up.

We brought our lunch to work. I think we ate while we were

working because I don't remember ever stopping the machine. It was hard work for the amount of money we got. But it was money and I was working. There were rats near the river. We could see them as we looked out the window.

One day I said to Frank what am I doing working in these mills? I've got a good education. I'm going back teaching. I had to take a course to get my teaching license back. So I took my course all summer long; it was a lot of work. But I loved it cause I knew I was going back into teaching. I taught in the Winooski public schools for twenty-three years.

Italians tended to live together. There were quite different areas too. Italians that lived near the Chace Mill were Rosetti and Franco on Barrett Street; Dattilio, Milizia and Cavarretta on Chase Street; Martello, Milizia, Pichierri on Grove Street; Franco on Mill Street; Trono Sr. on Colchester Avenue; Ponti, Michael Trono Sr. and Michael Trono Jr. on Richardson and Colchester Courts; Dattilio and Carrassi on Riverside Avenue (Lower Road). Mr. Pichierri had an Italian store on the corner of Colchester Avenue and Barrett Street. I can still see the steps you had to climb to get up to the door. Mr. Louis Doria was the next owner. Both sold Italian food. Mr. Doria had a small section where you could buy ice cream. The building is now Domino's Pizza. Italian men would meet in the store and reminisce about the old country. Loretta and Ernest Tatro had an Italian-American store in their home on Chase Street.

The one that stands out for me in Winooski was the Italian store located on Malletts Bay Avenue, just before you get to the railroad tracks. Mr. Cabrera (Spanish) and family sold imported Italian foods such as pasta by the pound, sausages, bread, olives, oils, different kinds of cheeses (mostly provolone), salami, canned tomatoes – everything Italian. If he didn't have it, he would order it. They used to break the pasta in half for you. It was about eighteen inches long. The building is still there. The Italian store is now Walt's Poolroom and at the other end is Trackside, a bar. There was another Italian store run by a Mr. Cosmo Doria on the corner of Weaver and West Allen Street. The Brigante family runs the vegetable farm on Malletts Bay Avenue.

Once you crossed the railroad tracks you were in "The Flats," a well known area in Winooski where most of the Italians lived. Families who lived here were Franco Arruzza on West Allen;

Corner of Follett and West Canal streets, across from the Woolen Mill.
Perrino's porch windows (upper right) overlook Madeline's corner garden.
*(Courtesy of Special Collections, University of Vermont Libraries)*

Giovanni Trono and Giovanni Perrino on West Canal; Franco
Mazzatelli, Domenic Scichitano, Michele DePaul and Guiseppi
Vartuli on Hickock Street; Salvatore Augostino, Francesco Pappilo,
Domenico Franze and Domenico Demasi on River Street;
Francesco Caforia, Guiseppe Ponessa, Michele Vartuli, Pietro
Brigante, Sam Brigante, Francesco Mazza, Bruno Gerace, Fiore
Mele and Tomas Rotella on Malletts Bay Avenue. Most of them
would walk to work in the mills.

Fort Pick, that's down Center Street (east of the Champlain
Mill). That's all gone now, demolished when they had the revital-
ization of Winooski. I thought it was Ford, F o r d, but my friend
Josie Arruzza told me it's Fort, F o r t. She says yes, because the
men from Fort Ethan Allen met a lot of the girls [from] down
there at dances held at the Fort. They could come from Fort Ethan
Allen and take the pick of the girl they wanted to go out with.

West Canal Street, that's what fascinated me when I was first
married. A little town like White River Junction, there wasn't too
much going on there, just a big railroad center. Then come here
and see these hundreds of people waiting on the streets to go to
work. It wasn't only Italians, but everyone would stop and talk
and laugh and smoke their cigarette. That was something I'd never

seen before and I loved it. I thought that was great, everyone together because usually you find the Irish in one place, the French in another place and the Italians in another place, but they would all talk to each other. Of course the workers would go into the Star Bakery and buy all their pastries because they used to make beautiful, oh wonderful pastries in there. My husband worked in this bakery.

The Italians went to St. Stephen's Church on Barlow Street. In the earlier days, other Catholics, primarily the Irish, attended St. Stephen's. They still call it the Irish Church. If you were French you went to the French church, Saint Francis Xavier, because they spoke French all the time. This has been changed for many years; English is now spoken. I see parishioners going to either church and it seems so good to see this. Korean, Vietnamese and Bosnian families are now members of St. Stephen's Parish.

There were many more French persons living in Winooski than Italians. The French settled up on the hill because that's where the French church is. I remember living in White River. The rich lived up on top of the hill. The rest lived down below. The children up on the hill were told not to go down there because of the Italians that lived there. Discrimination, yes, against the Italians. You could feel it. I didn't think there was any of that here [in Winooski]. However, after being married for a while, I found out there was friction between the children in the different areas.

*Madeline Perrino has lived with her husband, Frank, in an apartment across from the Woolen Mill for most of her fifty-nine years in Winooski. She has retired from teaching elementary school, but enjoys meeting her former students, one of whom is Gail Nicholas (essay on Syrians, p. 106). Currently, she is treasurer of the Winooski Historical Society.*

# The Polish in Winooski
## *Recollections of Connie Stech Flynn*

My name is Connie Stech Flynn. I live at 50 Follett Street in Winooski. And I've lived here all my life; it's really been a long time, I'm eighty-five. Nobody ever believes me, how old I am. I was born here. My mother and father married here. They didn't meet in Poland. They were born in Poland, yes. My mother, Mariana, was from Lubin. And my father, I can't remember. But if you know anything about Poland, evidently it's like a war place, I mean there was always a war there. For instance the Russians, the Germans, or somebody in the area.

Well the reason the Polish came is to make some money. Because they didn't have half the things, you know. I went to Poland in the 1960s. And do you know that we still didn't have refrigerators. They went outside, and they showed me where they had to put their meat. They dig hole about ten feet deep and put all the meat, they wrap it up and put in there to keep it. So we were way behind. I think we're just about the slowest country of any in Europe, in that area anyway.

I think other nationalities, they got farther, like the French and Italians. They did different things like stores. Very few of us had stores or anything like that. But we got

Mariana Stec at her home on West Allen Street c.1925. Later, Stec changed to Stech. *(Courtesy of Connie Stech Flynn)*

along; we had to do the best we could to live. It was very, very hard for the majority of the Polish people here. This is a small place anyway. The bigger cities, I guess they were a little better off than we are, but we live here. Winooski was here.

Oh yes, there were a lot of Polish people in Winooski, Stec which changed to Stech and Ignaszewski and Tolosky. Well, the majority of the people when they came over to this country would stay with relatives or somebody they know, to help them out. And through this they would get work. Through their relatives who were in the mills.

My mother worked in the mill and my father worked chopping wood. And he got sick. He was only thirty-four years old when he died. Had cancer. So, then my mother had us four to handle, she had three boys and myself. So she worked in the mill and gradually the boys worked in the mill as soon as they got to be sixteen.

The majority of the Polish people lived in the same neighborhood. Everybody would go to each other's house and the kids would all play together, you know the Polish kids. It was very interesting to see how they lived and how they tried, and how everybody saved money and everybody practically got together. Very few Italians were in this area because they had more money. There were a lot of them. They had businesses like restaurants. And the Polish people, we didn't have that. We had to work in the mills to make any money where the Italians, right away they get a store so they were far ahead of us.

Further down the street they had an apartment house and Polish people owned that. They came from Canada. Years ago a lot of people came that way from Canada. Anybody that could get into Canada, they finally got in here. See that was a shortcut. Say I was working in the mill and you happened to be maybe my cousin. So you'd come over to see me and first thing you know you'd be in the United States.

They lived as boarders, they settled, they'd meet a friend and they'd get a job. Somebody must have been over here and said that there was a mill here, well, between one person to another. At one time, my mother had about five boarders. They came over to get jobs and then they stayed at our house, maybe they even stuck three in a bed, you know till they found something. Because it was hard finding things if you can't speak English. But they were all close, very, very close.

The Polish people lived in blocks. Did they ever tell you that all these houses are built by the mill? The mill had a store that you could go there and buy things on credit till you got the money. No interest. Then there was the houses, you paid the rent to the mill.

And that's about the only way they lived until they got money enough that they bought something. This house, the majority of the houses in this area, and you go down near the street where Mrs. Perrino lives [West Allen across from the Woolen Mill], all that was mill. I mean the mill people. This is where they lived. But all this was mostly Polish. And so [my mother] lived there and then she had a chance to buy a house so she did, way down the street.

Connie Stech Flynn in front of her childhood home on West Allen Street, 1999.

We had our garden in our back yard. We had everything in our garden. My mother canned. We used to can just about everything that we could, beets and carrots and corn and just everything. My mother had a cow and a pig. Because my father died, she built a nice barn out there. And we had apple trees, pear trees, we had grapes and we had everything. My mother didn't have to buy anything practically. We had tomatoes. You know we had tomatoes down the cellar. When she died she had about three hundred jars of tomatoes. We never went to the store to get a can of anything. Anytime you wanted anything you just went down the cellar.

A majority of us ate Polish foods. Well, I think you probably heard of one of those things, cabbage rolls. You cook rice, and some people used to grind ham, most of the people, it was beef. And of course you added an egg and you added different things to keep it together. You buy a nice cabbage and you take the leaves off; you part them and put them in water and let them come to a boil because they had to be flexible to roll them, and then you roll them in. And that is the worst thing. I hate to make them now. Everybody, they come and want me to make 'em. I tell you, the priest and everybody else, oh please make 'em. They don't understand that you gotta be careful of the kind of cabbage you buy, because if it's got a little hole in it, cabbage beetle in there, then they tear. A lot of people liked the different Polish foods. Particularly in breads, braided breads and raisin breads. Even when my brothers were older and married, for Easter I made them all a small loaf because I had three brothers. You know the Kabosh, that's Polish sausage and we used to make that.

My mother was the most stubborn woman in the world. She figured she was born Polish and she's gonna die Polish. She didn't wanna speak English at all. I'd have to go to the doctor's with her when I was about nine years old. Because by that time I had gone to school and I understood a few things. She got around, like in the mill. Course they didn't visit that much, they didn't have time. My father died when I was eight years old and I was the oldest. So she had to come home and make meals for the next day so she didn't have too much time to visit.

She didn't ever want to go back to Poland. She was only about eighteen or nineteen years old when she came here. Her father brought her over. Her father used to be on a boat and he used to bring everyone. But my father, I never could remember how he learned English and she didn't. She was still awful stubborn. We'd come in the house and our prayers and everything were all said in Polish. Everything was Polish.

We all belonged to St. Stephens Church. They had a French church here. They have masses in English too but it used to be French. We had a few Irish around the Polish people down where I lived. They built the Irish church, that's St. Stephens. And Father McGarry, way back then, he's the one that started it and that's where we all went to church. See, so it's much easier for us. The Polish priest from Rutland would come to Winooski and then all the Polish people would go to Confession and Communion. Our parents had to wait once a year to go to confession. Once a year at Easter time.

Pretty many holidays that we had, but our main one was Easter. I guess it was cause they were very religious, all Polish people were. It meant so much that Christ was risen, that was better than the Christmas tree. It just seems when Christ died and He came, you know Resurrection again, all that was very important. And we didn't eat meat on Friday. My mother would buy us cans of sardines on New Year's Eve cause we couldn't eat meat. Because we kinda liked that cause it was bought.

We had a lot of dances in our own homes. They were in the kitchens, whoever had the biggest kitchen. That's how we really would have our good times. We always had Polish dances. A fiddler came and fiddled. It's just the same like a birthday or

St. Stephens Church built in 1872. This church was replaced in 1928. *(Adapted from a photograph, c. early 1900s, courtesy of Winooski Historical Society)*

a christening or things like that. That's what you had a lot of, dancing. Because that's all they had would be somebody that could play a fiddle. We had special good times and dancing, polkas. I used to dance the polka when I was eight years old. We'd have something to eat. Cakes, whatever. Like I say, we were big on breads, raisin breads, and oh beautiful breads. I'm telling you I used to love the breads. Everybody did.

We spoke Polish, naturally until we started school, and the people worked in the mill. But before that all we spoke was Polish. We couldn't talk English in the house and it made it hard for us in school. I went to the public school; there isn't a Polish Catholic school here. The nearest one would be Rutland. I could not speak a word in English when I went to school. In fact when I was at school I had to go to a room where it contained Polish people so they could explain to the teacher what I wanted, even going to the bathroom. This is how bad it was.

I went to school till the sophomore year in high school. Then my mother wanted me to go in the mill cause I was about thirteen or fourteen years old. I did get a job. Then the boss found out I wasn't of age so he threw me out. He just told me I would never get a job in the mill again. I did a lot of things wherever you could work, housework or whatever you could do. But I really wanted to go to school. I just made it till the sophomore year.

We'd get one job and it would run out, then we'd have to go look for another job or housework. And when it slacked down a little bit, the factories, a lot of the Polish people went to New

Hampshire. My mother went, but she didn't like it very well because she had to leave us kids. But then a lot of the Polish people got smarter. We had Polish bosses; we had Mr. Ignaszewski, Peter. I don't know where he got educated, because we met him when he was already a boss in the mill. So he gave Polish people a break. If he could hire a Polish person he did, and got 'em jobs, but finally everybody got out on their own.

Well I did work at the mill. We used to pick up all the rags. And I mean by rags, everything was wool at one time. The Jewish people used to go around in carts, a horse and buggy, and pick up all the rags. And they preferred that we had the linings out, you see. All those rags, so they'd bring them to the mill. They washed them in great big barrels, wooden big things. Then they put them to a machine to dust them. They were really clean. They made sure we didn't get sick or anything.

Then we sorted them for color. Dark colors we had to put aside. We were taught to put blue with the light blue stuff, you know how years ago you had to put a little bit of bluing to whiten it. This is what I did for quite a few years. And they if didn't have work in what they called this old mill, then they had what they called the new mill, the Champlain Mill, because it was built later. The bosses would shove me around just to keep me working.

*Among her many jobs, Connie Stech Flynn has also worked as a hair dresser. She likes to get out, to be with people and is still very active in her community. She volunteers at the Fanny Allen Hospital gift shop several days a week, maintains her own home and continues to attend St. Stephens Church.*

# The Armenians
## *Recollections of Lucy (Lucia), Edward (Haig) and Steve Boyajian*

*The Boyajians, an Armenian immigrant family, lived in the shadow of the Winooski Falls mills. Lucy and her brothers, Edward and Steve, recount their parents' escape from persecution, their settlement in Burlington, their struggles and rewards in a mill town, and the cultural traditions the family maintained.*

### Emigration

*Steve:* My father came to this country early in the 1920s. He knew what was going to happen before the Turkish massacre started. They had conscription where they used to draft Armenian people into the Turkish army to fight against their own people. I mean when the massacres were going on. My father escaped twice from the Turkish army. I think the second time he escaped he managed to leave the country. He headed to Marseilles, France, and from there he went to Lowell and Lawrence, Massachusetts, just wherever there was work. He worked in a shoe factory, but he

The Boyajian home at the south end of the Winooski-Burlington Bridge just after the 1927 flood. The first story became a second basement when the grade on the west side was raised to accommodate the height of the new bridge. The building, built between 1841 and 1846 as a store, later served as a forge, a blacksmith shop and a wheelwright shop. From 1884 to 1912 it was a second-hand store. The Boyajians acquired it in 1922. The Champlain Mill is partly visible on the left. *(Courtesy of Special Collections, University of Vermont Libraries)*

spent most of his time in the textile mills. From there he went to Madison, Maine, the textile mills in Maine, and then finally he settled here [Burlington] because of friends. How he made it there I don't know.

I think all the Armenians here [left Armenia because of] the persecution, absolutely. Some of them came from my father's hometown in Armenia, so there were friends, some of them very close friends. It was called Chermoog; it was south of Yerevan which is the capital.

*Lucy:* My mother was a victim of the Turkish massacres. Her mother threw herself into the Euphrates River because she knew the Turks were coming. My mother was left in an orphanage. I think she was in Syria. Through acquaintances and friends, my father started writing letters and sending money to help her. One thing led to another and eventually he brought her over to this country. They met in Cuba, actually got married in Cuba, and then he brought her to Burlington.

Naturally, [our parents] spoke Armenian. They also spoke some Turkish because of the occupation of the Turks in their homeland. [We speak] broken Armenian. We don't [speak Turkish], we don't care to. But [our parents] had to, and when they didn't want us to understand something, they spoke Turkish. We couldn't understand anything they were talking about. They were immigrants. They could speak three languages, not fluently: Turkish, broken English and Armenian.

*Lucy:* The first part of an Armenian name has significance to profession or family history, and the "ian" signifies "the family of." Boyajian, which is our name, were people who did dye work. Some Winooski Armenians were Bedrosian, Sam Moroian (Green Mountain Lunch), Gabriel Kaprielian, George Esperian (mill elevator operator), Harry Krikorian (weaver), and Harry Kevorkian (barber).

*Edward:* Harry the Barber gave the greatest haircuts. His last name was Kevorkian, Harry Kevorkian. His barbershop was right up above Green Mountain Lunch. I'd go in there to get my hair cut [for 25 cents] and there'd be a lot of the French people in there getting their hair cut from Harry the Barber. There were several barbershops in Winooski [run by] French people. Harry the Barber, he was good.

## Festivals

A lot of the Armenian families used to go up to Sand Bar State Park. We used to have a lot of picnics up there, just about every weekend. Mount Mansfield State Park too, and we used to go down to North Beach. Those three places were pretty popular. Even though we didn't live next door to each other, we were pretty clannish. Oh, they'd all get together, just like the Italians and everybody else.

*Lucy:* Easter [was important]. My mother always dyed the Easter eggs in onion peels. That was a traditional thing. Of course, the dessert was the popular *paklava*. It's similar to *baklava*.

Food, that's the best part. We have the best food. We make our traditional Easter rolls; we call them *Cheoregs*. We grew up making those. It kind of reminds us of home, watching our mom make it. During the winter, my brothers and I helped. And we do stuffed grape leaves. We pick our own leaves. We make a lot of those. We make a meat shell stuffed with another type of meat mixture. A lot of stews. Cooking is a very important part of the home life. It took hours to do, because of the individual portions.

*Edward:* The Armenians have a very long history of the Christian religion. Armenia was the first nation to adopt Christianity. It's the national religion and a very important part of our culture. In fact, this upcoming year they'll be celebrating their 1700th anniversary, seventeen hundred years!

The closest church to Armenian Orthodox was St. Paul's, that's where we were baptized, St. Paul's Episcopal Church in Burlington. I was never much of a church-goer, but Ma used to go to what they called the Irish church, St. Stephens. She used to come home with the palms and stuff. I used to go once in a while.

## The Mills

*Edward:* [During] World War II these mills ran constantly, seven days a week. In shifts, never stopped. We could hear the looms all the time when we lived across the river there. It was strange, sometimes we wouldn't hear these looms running, we thought it was going to be the end of the world. That's how used to it [we were]. We used to go to sleep by that. It's like a serenade. Clackity clack clackity clack clackity clack, like a train on the railroad tracks. Standing outside the house, you could hear it just as plain as could be. Especially at the river. [The river] would carry the

Clockwise: Cheoreg (yeast rolls), Bastegh (fruit leather), Tel Khadayef (shredded walnut-filled pastry), roasted pumpkin seeds, Beoreg (cheese-filled rolls), Leblebou (parched peas), Shish-Kebab (barbecued lamb) and Kufta (stuffed meat balls), string cheese, Yalanchi (stuffed grape leaves), Paklava (dessert), nut-filled pastry, Katah (buttered coffee bread). *(Courtesy of Lucy Boyajian)*

sound. Every day at 2:30 I remember hearing the whistle blow which meant that shift was over. Then people would leave.

*Lucy:* I believe the whistle was over at the woolen mill side. It blew at 6:30 in the morning and 2:30 in the afternoon. It didn't blow at night. I guess they didn't want to wake up people.

*Edward:* I remember the trucks coming in with raw cotton. Cotton and wool. Unloading bales of it. It would be processed over at the [Chace Mill] first and then brought over to this [Champlain] mill. This was mostly all worsted here, and nylon too. We made automobile cloth on this side, with a lot of nylon in it.

*Steve:* To get extra money, we would go along the [river] banks and pick up Coke bottles. Two cents apiece we'd get. If we couldn't find any in the grass, we'd look up and the people'd be looking at us that were working in the mill. We'd say, "Hey, how about throwing us some Coke bottles?" They'd throw a few Coke bottles to us. We'd get enough together; we'd cash 'em in. That was our way for getting our money for our candy and popsicles and what not, from Coke bottles.

We used to collect the brass and copper off the shuttles. When they had parts that were no longer of use, the truck would gather it from the mills and they'd go up in back of Chace Mill, where the power plant is now, and they'd burn it. The shuttles are wood and there's either brass or copper on both ends. We would wait till the fire died down, then we'd go sifting through and get all the brass and copper. We were just like eagles; we were pros after a while. I could have identified brass and copper a mile away. When we'd get enough of it, this person from Winooski would buy it from us. We'd just watch for that truck to come over. They'd come over at least once or twice a week.. That's what we did to stay out of trouble. It was quite an experience. Oh, Jesus, [we were] probably seven, eight years old, to ten to twelve years old. In the 1930s.

*Edward:* They [mill workers] were mostly all French. A few Irish. I had no problems [being Armenian], no. I was a good worker and that's all they seemed to care about. I worked hard and I saved my money. We were paid in cash. Paymaster would come around every Friday. He'd have this belt buckled with envelopes in it, all individual envelopes. People would be in the mill here, up and down and everywhere. He'd pull out their envelope and give it to them. Strictly cash and each envelope had their deduction and so on.

*Edward:* When I first started, my pay was something like $44 a week. 1951. My first job was associated with the weave room. Then they took me off and put me on the winders which was a couple dollars a week difference in pay. So it was still around $40 for at least 40 hours. But I heard the ones [that] had better jobs were the weavers; the weavers made good money. Those that worked overtime would come home – everybody would talk about "Oh, you made $80 this week." [Our father] he did weaving. He was strictly a weaver, that's what he was. I remember [him] bringing home $60, $70. Everything was cash. He'd [my father] come home with three twenty-dollar bills, and sometimes four twenty-dollar bills, and he felt like a lord. We all got new shoes. That was big money back then, $80, wow! This was in the late thirties.

*Steve:* My father couldn't read or write. Pa could write his name. But my mother, she could read and write some. She got some education here, my mother did. She went to night school. My mother never worked. She was a homemaker.

My father owned properties over there [near the Chace Mill]. He had two partners; two Armenian friends of his together bought those two buildings. I remember [his] telling about having to fix this pipe and that, because they didn't have the money to hire a plumber. That broke and this broke. You'd have to become a plumber, a carpenter and electrician and everything, cause he didn't have the money to hire help. Plus working in the mill, he was collecting rents. It wasn't easy.

# The Syrians and the Mill
## by Gail A. Nicholas

Most of the Syrian families came to Winooski around 1912, after first joining family and friends who had come before them, settling in Glens Falls, Geneva, and Massena, New York; and Wilkes Barre, Pennsylvania. A number of Lebanese came from North Adams, Massachusetts. Each group came to Winooski seeking jobs at the American Woolen Company on the advice of those who had already settled here.

Abraham Nicholas, from Wilkes Barre, worked in the picking room, where wool was graded, and in the dye house with Michael Abraham, from Michigan, whose wife Lizzie was a winder. Abraham and Samuel Leo from Massena worked in the card room. The Jacobs family, George and Thomas from Standish, New York, and their cousin Louis, from Glens Falls, were weavers as were Anna Tamer and Arthur Tamer, who were Lebanese. Joseph Tamer worked with Michael Leo in wet finish. Many Lebanese worked in the spinning and twisting departments. John and George Leo were in the spinning department. Nicholas Nicholas was a loom fixer. *[A son named Nicholas is called Nicholas Nicholas if he is the son of Nicholas. The real family name is left unsaid.]*

The women, Sarah Leo, Helen Nicholas, Mary Nicholas Jacobs, Lizzie Abraham, Anna Moses Jacobs and Adra John, were mainly in twisting and winding. Most of the women worked the second shift, affording those who were married the opportunity to get their children off to school and to tend to household tasks, including food preparation for the day. The fathers would be home when the children returned from school. They would see that the children were fed, that their homework was done and that they were put to bed. Both parents were always working, either in the home or in the mill.

The first-generation Syrian immigrants worked until the Winooski mills closed in 1954. Most of the children of the Syrian and Lebanese immigrants worked in the woolen trade as well. During the 1940s, many worked as many as sixteen hours a day to aid the war effort. After the war, the women stayed on, but some of the men who had been in the service furthered their education through the GI Bill of Rights.

The Syrians were never strangers to hard work. In Syria, they had only themselves to depend on for their survival. They worked long hours in the fields to provide for their families. They saw America as a place where they could work to achieve more than mere survival, a place where their children would learn how to provide a better existence for themselves.

Zara Nicholas Jacobs, Mary Nicholas Moses, Abraham Nicholas, Mary Nicholas, c.mid 1900s. *(Courtesy of Gail Nicholas)*

Most first-generation Syrians in Winooski did not become proficient in English. They did stress to their children the need to assimilate into American culture by learning English, and by getting the best education they could. In Syria at this time not many were being educated; women were not even allowed to attend school. So these new immigrants were "progressive" by encouraging their children to better themselves. We spoke Arabic at home. I spoke it, but the script was difficult. Not many had command of the written language. Arabic is written from right to left and books begin at the back.

The Syrians were Syrian Orthodox Christians. Since no Orthodox church was available here, the Orthodox bishop from Boston would come once a month to give them communion. The Episcopalians let the Syrians use their church for services. After the bishop could no longer make these trips, they became Episcopalians. They loved and cared for their new church and became fast friends with its congregation. The younger Syrian children were baptized Episcopalian.

The Syrians lived in clusters, primarily near the Woolen Mill. Eventually some moved to the West End, from rental properties to their own homes, a move that signified their success. They still remained in small clusters, living, working and helping each other.

In summer we would go to Sand Bar Beach State Park for picnics – there might be thirty-five of us. Arabic dishes included homemade "pita" bread, rolled grape leaves stuffed with rice and hamburger or lamb, and *Koosa*, Syrian zucchini which is hollowed out with a special utensil, stuffed as a green pepper would be, and boiled in tomatoes. They prepared *Kibbee Sin-ee-yah*, trays of meat, crushed

Trinity Episcopal Mission Church, 1877. (Adapted from *Look Around Winooski, Vermont,* with permission of Chittenden County Historical Society)

wheat and onions that were baked and cut into diamond shapes. They brought *Shyreyea*, a rice egg noodle, chickpea and chicken dish, in large kettles to serve with cooked tomatoes, onions and string beans. Some vegetarian dishes were *Imjadara*, lentils and rice, and *Marshushee*, spinach and crushed wheat.

The Syrians were resourceful people. The men fished the Winooski River and Lake Champlain. For heating and cooking fuel, they collected driftwood along the riverbank, scrap wood from Porter Screen Shop and Vermont Furniture Factory, and waste wood from the Woolen Mill. The women and children gathered berries; some even sold them for extra money. They picked grape leaves that grew wild for traditional Syrian recipes.

Gardens were very important to the Syrians, Lebanese and other immigrants as a supplement to their mill earnings. The entire family tended them. Each family helped the other if a certain crop had failed one of them. Some of their socializing was going from one house to the other to help with the harvest and food-processing. They became good friends with the Italians, Poles and French in their neighborhood. Everyone seemed to have the same life style at that time.

During the summer months the children would fight among themselves as to which one of them would bring their father his lunch at the mill. All knew the lucky one would be rewarded with a five-cent bottle of cold Coke from the vending machine. They would state their business for entering the mill to Michael Arruzza, the

Italian security guard whom they knew from their neighborhood.

All found honor in working in a foreign land, even in the most menial jobs. They were thankful to have the opportunities and freedom that America offered. They came to a culture completely foreign to them; they learned and assimilated. They were loved and respected by their old friends and their new neighbors. To this day we still remain friends with the other immigrant families in the old neighborhood and we stay in touch with the Syrians who have moved away. The memories and stories of our ancestors have taught us the value of hard work and of being good friends and neighbors.

*Gail A. Nicholas grew up in Winooski, a third-generation member of the Syrian community. She has a bachelor's degree in political science from the University of Vermont. She has worked in the United State Senate, and for both Governor Richard Snelling and Lieutenant Governor Barbara Snelling; she has also been a development director for non-profit organizations. She lives in Essex Junction, Vermont.*

# A Syrian Immigrant Family
## *Recollections of Nicholas Morwood*

I love this country because it is the land of opportunity. The Syrians, along with other nationalities, came to the United States to find a better life. We see this happening even today. Cubans, Haitians, Mexicans and Chinese are dying in an effort to immigrate to this country. An old Polish lady, herself an immigrant, once said to me that no one need be poor in this country, but they had to be willing to work.

My parents had nothing to look forward to [in Syria], except as being dirt farmers. My mother came from [the village of] Dware Taha about 1910 when she was ten or eleven years old. She came over with her older brother who was only about two years older than she was. My father came from Melka in about 1900. They met and married in Winooski.

I've lived in Winooski all my life even though I was born in Michigan. [My] family lived on East Allen Street, the "Fort Pick" [apartments] *(next to the Champlain Mill)* and [later] on West Allen Street. West Allen Street was called Cork Alley because many of the Irish who lived on the street came from County Cork in Ireland. I remodeled the 150-year-old family home and live on Cork Alley now.

[My parents] worked in the American Woolen Company, my mother as a winder and my father in the dye house. I worked there as a bobbin boy during two high school vacations. My father was offered a job as a foreman but he had to refuse because he couldn't read or write. Neither could my mother.

Lizzie Abraham (left) and Mike Abraham (right), Nicholas (Abraham) Morwood's parents c.1950. *(Courtesy of Nicholas Morwood)*

My father told me that Syria was part of the Ottoman Empire when he was a boy, that when the Turkish horsemen came to his village all the boys ran into the hills. They didn't want to be beaten up and they didn't want to be recruited into the Turkish army. The Turks might have been the reason to get out. He said the Turks were mean to the people.

I have to give them, and all other immigrants, a great deal of credit for having the ambition to better themselves. They came to this country without knowing the language, without money, and without connections other than a friend who preceded them.

Abraham homestead on West Allen St. *(From* Look Around Winooski, Vermont, *with permission of Chittenden County Historical Society)*

This is the American way: My parents who could neither read nor write brought up three children, a lawyer, an engineer and a merchant. The three boys all served in the armed services. I was in the army, George was in the air force and Jim was in the navy. George served in World War II and the Korean War. He visited relatives in Syria while on furlough during World War II. I have a lawyer, a psychiatrist, a plastic surgeon, a teacher and two secretaries as children. I tell my kids that they've got to do better than I have, because they've got every advantage.

*Nicholas Morwood is an attorney in South Burlington. He graduated from high school in 1933 during the depression, when there was no money for college. He studied in a law office, was admitted to the bar in 1938, and spent three and one-half years in the U.S. Army during World War II. He has served Winooski as a Grand Juror, a councilman, a Planning Commission member, as Model Cities chairman, and was on the Vermont Real Estate Commission for seventeen years.*

## Lebanese Traditions
### *Recollections of Larry Handy*

My name is Larry Handy. I was born and brought up in Winooski. Born 1930, March 17 on East Allen Street. The house still stands. My father was an immigrant from Lebanon, the town known as Wadi Kannoubin. (Wadi in Arabic means town.) It's in the northern part of Lebanon, in a valley. They didn't have hot and cold running water [or] flush toilets. There wasn't much opportunity. Life was rather stagnant. You were born, you lived and you died. And not much in between. The incentives or the ability to make a difference in Lebanon wasn't the same. You were either born of opportunity and born of means or you did not.

My mother was born here in America. Her mother and father, however, did migrate from Lebanon. They lived in Newport, Vermont. As a matter of fact my mother was a Hendy before she married a Handy. Most marriages during that time were arranged within the family. My wife happens to be French, O.K., but I'm from the modern era as opposed to those that had recently migrated from the old country. All your social functions, all the activity, all the get-together was mostly among members of the family. They were comfortable that way because they had more in common. [Like] those that had migrated, say from Canada or Armenia or wherever else. And it

Joe, Cecile, Larry, Jennie and Floyd Handy c. 1934. Joe Handy was in the ice and coal business. He used to carry huge blocks of ice over his shoulder; he would complain when he had to walk up two stories with such a weight. Background: Huard Photo Studio, Winooski. *(Courtesy of Gail Wyand)*

continued to be that way until World War II.

My wife Lorraine is a Burlington girl. Her name was Viau, a prominent French family in the Burlington region. She lived across the street from the Jewish synagogue on Archibald Street. When I first became engaged to her, it was tradition that your wife meet the seniors of the family for their approval. The matriarch of the family lived in Lyndonville. Her name is Aunt Mariani, that's Marion. So my mother is introducing my wife Lorraine to my Aunt Mariani, and my Aunt Mariani says to my mother, *binant*, American or Arab? And my mother responded, she says *binant*, American. And my Aunt Mariani went tsk, tsk, tsk, tsk. Too bad, too bad. Of course my wife was a little provoked to find the fact that she was French didn't meet with Aunt Marion's approval. But that was the attitude back then.

We used to kid each other on how, oh heck, I've got cousins that married where the fathers were brothers and the mothers were sisters. And the first born of each married. Now that's pretty close. My wife used to say well, aren't any of 'em loony? And my mother would turn, she says, I married my cousin, was I loony? My mother was really offended by that, you know, thinking incest and all that kind of thing. But they weren't. That was tradition back then. You married within the family and that was it.

It wasn't only true with the Lebanese. It was true with all the families, French included. I know French families, even now, where the spouses were related prior to marriage.

When World War II came around, things changed. Young men went into the service; they went to all parts of the country besides all parts of the world and discovered there were other young ladies and other young men who were other nationalities. It was not isolated to just the nationality that you happened to be born to. That's really what being American was all about.

Even though we were in Winooski, in America, we continued to eat Mediterranean foods. They were never high on food that was made A-mer-i-can. We had a [Lebanese] dish that was rather delicious, that was made with raw meat, raw beef (in the old country lamb was common), very lean with crushed wheat and spices; when it was made for the first time, you ate it raw still to this day. That dish is known as *Kibbee*. Even my wife who is French learned from my mother how to prepare all of these Arabic and Mideast dishes.

As to our livelihood, my father was the iceman in Winooski for fifty years. He bought the ice business, the Gilbrook Ice Company. Later, to keep himself occupied through the winter, they added coal. So then [it] became known as the Gilbrook Coal and Ice Company. We handled coal in the wintertime and ice in the summertime. The flood [in] 1927 took away the icehouse. [It] used to be right across from the Champlain Mill. A new icehouse was built where Gilbrook Pond is today. Gilbrook Pond used to be the reservoir for Winooski. Two ponds are still there. As you go up Interstate 89, north of Winooski, on the right, you'll see where the Winooski municipal garage is and adjacent to it there's an upper pond and a lower pond. We used to harvest ice there. We harvested some [ice] from the river, but we harvested most from Malletts Bay on Lake Champlain.

You'd wonder why people from such a nice climate as Lebanon would settle in Vermont and be in the ice business. I suppose, as long as you went to America, wherever you ended up opportunity existed. Maybe the first ones that came to America happened to settle in Vermont and didn't really have any idea. But be that as it was, we learned a little bit about the ice and coal business. We grew up in the business. Like the farm boys who went to school there, we worked in the business, only we were needed in the wintertime to help harvest ice. It was family occupation. We had to work cause they needed our effort and our energy. We used to miss a lot of school in the wintertime. It's a wonder we ever got out of eighth grade, no less got out of college.

That was another thing with our family background. They believed strongly in education, because without education you were a failure. Which really wasn't true. You could succeed in America without an education. But we had to have an education. So, myself and my brother and my sister got an education. I went to the Protestant schools. My mother always referred to the public schools as the Protestant schools. You know, the public schools in Winooski: Winooski Grammar School, Winooski High School, Norwich University.

But we had religion at the Protestant schools. They brought the nuns. Many of the kids went to the "Morial" school, as we used to call it, we left out the m e m and called it the Morial school instead of the Memorial. Many of the kids that went to the Memorial school from the sixth grade on were from St. Francis

Xavier. I suppose it made a difference as to where you lived in Winooski. And we walked back and forth to school. No school busses or anything like that. We used to get

Left to right: unknown, Ernie Handy, brother George Handy, and unknown, c. 1940. George Handy, Burlington ice dealer, married Cecile Handy, a distant cousin, of the Winooski Gilbrook Ice & Coal Company family. George later ran George's restaurant in Burlington. *(Courtesy of Gail Wyand)*

the nuns from St. Mary's or Cathedral. They used to come every week right into the public schools and teach religion to the Catholics.

I think your behavior, your social behavior, was a result of your religious training. Girl-boy behavior, for example. In the neighborhood I grew up in, most of the kids that we played with, socialized with, were all of the same feeling, and most of our friends were Catholic too, so it wasn't [all Lebanese]. No, no, mostly French. There were some spots where the Italians were clustered a little bit.

Of course, we're Catholic. Winooski had two Catholic churches, Saint Francis Xavier and St. Stephens. St. Stephens was always called the Irish church. I suppose mostly because Father McGarry was its original pastor. He was Irish. I've always, in amusement, questioned how so few Irish families in Winooski, you can see the power of the Irish, managed to get a church designated as the Irish church in the community probably ninety-eight percent French. The Lebanese who lived in Winooski went to St. Stephens.

We were so religious. After supper, it was almost routine, you went to the living room, kneeled down, said the prayers. Especially during ice harvesting time, so we'd have success. The practice of religion was an integral part of our daily lives. We lived according to the ritual, the Holy Days, no meat on Friday, church on Sunday, First Friday, confession, that kind of thing. Sometimes I think it was overdone, but it was a doctrine that you were just so routinely adapted to that it was a matter of fact.

Religion played a big part in our lives. For example, my father's father was a Catholic priest [who] migrated to America and was a priest for the Lebanese community [in] Burlington. His parish was the chapel at the old Cathedral church. He was multilingual like the Pope, because if you went into religious life, you got an enormous education, if you did not, you got very little education.

My grandfather was a married priest. My grandmother died soon after the last child was born. I think it was Bishop Rice that told my grandfather you can continue to do your priestly duties for as long as you agree to never remarry. Of course he never remarried. [The bishop] took a liking to my grandfather because I guess the wisdom my grandfather had; his ability to be multilingual impressed the bishop. I think it was 1922, there was the big flu epidemic then. He did [go] back to Lebanon to pay a visit.

Then I guess the bishop sent for him to come back to Burlington, Vermont, because his flock needed attention. They were having a hard time to communicate because the priests here [didn't] speak Lebanese. It was tough. Of course, they were very religious people, so my grandfather did come back. Then the children followed, my father, his two brothers and two sisters. [They worshipped] in Cathedral church.

My grandfather, the priest, spelled his name Hendy. My father spelled his name Handy along with his brother-in-law and sister. His other two brothers spelled their names Hendy. [On] my mother's side of the family, who was also Handy, her father spelled his name Hendy. The story goes that Hendy was the original spelling. But there's still family back in Lebanon whose name is spelled Handy. We have Handys and Hendys who could be brother and sister or two brothers.

In the old country it didn't make any difference how you spelled your last name. You didn't receive any mail. Also, if you had a son in the old country you always managed to name your son Joseph, either his surname or middle name, after the patron saint, St. Joseph. So they're all named Joe. In the old country it didn't mean a hill of beans of difference. But now they're in America and they're getting mail. Maybe just an ad, and it says to Joseph Hendy, and they'd fight tooth and nail as to who that belonged to. And so one says, hey, I'm gonna spell my name H a n d y. And whatever comes Handy belongs to me. And what ever comes H e n d y, Joe Hendy, belongs to you. That's OK when it was just two.

Then there were four and eight and ten and fifteen and fifty and sixty and one hundred and two hundred. I believe the original spelling is Hendy.

I enjoyed growing up in Winooski. At home we spoke mostly Arabic, as my French friends had spoken mostly French at home. If you were my French friend, and I brought you home with me, and my mother or my dad talked to me in Arabic or Lebanese, after you left I would tell them, don't you do that anymore. You speak English. You know how, you speak English. Especially in front of my friends, you speak English, not Arabic. I don't want them to think that we're talking about them. It was no different than [their] parents talking to them in French when I was at their house.

Oh, language was key. My father could speak French as well as English and Arabic. Not only that, he could speak Italian too, because the one thing you learned in school in the old country was language. And if you were being trained to be a priest, you even had more emphasis on language. I spoke a little French. My wife is French. I had French in school, and most of my friends were French. Matter of fact, I had a Polish friend, Ignaszewski. I think he still lives in the area. Name is Leon Ignaszewski. They're a Polish family that grew up in Winooski.

I think both they and us [Lebanese, French, etc.] were [in] so much of a hurry to become Americanized that we lost the value of learning to speak another language. We learned the cultures, the foods and most everything else dealing with the habits of our native culture but we somehow were embarrassed by letting our American friends be exposed to our origin. My father used to say never be ashamed of your nationality. And I never was. I was awfully proud being Lebanese and Arab. But I was somewhat embarrassed I suppose, because you know your father came from the old country who talked with an accent. I don't think it was any different for us than it was for the other kids.

There weren't that many Lebanese in Winooski, and sometimes they would refer to Lebanese as being Syrian, and the only thing they had in common was language. Arabic. To a degree, Lebanese were somewhat insulted being referred to as Syrian, you see. That was something that was transported from the old country. The Syrians and the Lebanese in the old country didn't have much love [for] each other. I think that's still true today.

We lived in that two-tenement house, 268 East Allen Street, that's just above the railroad tracks as you go up East Allen Street. Between the first house on top of that hill and 268 was a ravine that was used as a city dump. That used to be our playground. When somebody brought fresh dumpings, we kids who lived there used to yell out: I got first pickings, I got first pickings. Course the kid that had the fastest legs could run the fastest is the one that had first pickings. You could yell it out, but if you weren't there first, you didn't have first pickings.

The owner of the house was Mose Kerkorian. During the course of the year, the upstairs was always warmer during the wintertime and the downstairs was always cooler in the summertime. I'm not sure if there are any Kerkorians left in Winooski, but he was Armenian and an immigrant like my father. When fall would come, he'd get a hold of my father and say, hey a Joe, and my father'd say, yes Mose. He says, you moofa downstairs, I moofa up a stairs. And we moved down a stairs. And come springtime, he'd get a hold of my father again and say, hey Joe, you moofa up a stairs, I moofa down a stairs. Well, who besides two immigrants would have the nerve to consistently insist, cause you own the house, that the tenant would live downstairs during the winter months, and upstairs during the summer months. But they didn't mind. They were all happy enough to have a roof over their heads. And the rent never changed. I think the rent at the time was about $7 a month. House ownership back then was rather unique. Not many people owned the house that they lived in.

In 1937 my dad bought a piece of land up the street. So, in 1937 Dad built the house, the same house that was moved when the interstate highway came in. The bridge that crosses East Allen Street was where our house was. My dad in his attachment to the house paid the fee to prevent its demolition, and moved it. The house still stands there. Brother and I [own it now]. There's thirteen apartments there, it's the building just below the hill from St. Michael's College.

Most Winooski people were pretty much alike. All struggling to survive. All working to provide the necessities of life for themselves and their families. You never had to worry about the class society system. American Woolen played a big part; almost everyone living in Winooski had some connection with American Woolen directly or indirectly. [If] you were in business, you did business with people who worked at American Woolen. So, their employment at American Woolen made a difference between whether your business succeeded or did not, or whether you got paid for your service or product or did not. American Woolen, I think, touched just about everybody's life in Winooski at one point in time.

John O'Brien, he's the only manager that most of us knew and I knew his children. I knew Bill who's a lawyer and Bob who's a doctor. Their children were just as humble and as localized and street people as we were. So the kids managed to get along. They weren't looked upon as the upper strata of Winooski society cause there wasn't any upper strata of Winooski society. But they were highly respected by virtue of being boss of the mill, so that give you a position that not many people had.

There were quite a few [Lebanese] that [worked in the mills]. There wasn't [any] other occupation then, other than the mill to work in. It was American Woolen. A lot of the young people after graduation just automatically would go work for American Woolen. And retire from American Woolen. When American Woolen left Winooski, it was really tough. Depression set in. How are we gonna survive? What's going to happen? But they managed. Now most people who live there have persevered and found alternatives, and other industries came to town. There was a low period when things looked bad and bleak. I suppose you become better from it. My father's brother's son ran for mayor of Winooski. Fred, he was president of the union at American Woolen at one time, and he ran a restaurant on Main Street, the Deluxe.

[When] we grew older, and [were] out of school looking for occupation[s], we ended up coming to Swanton, Vermont. Dad had a trucking business that he had started and did trucking exclusively for Swanton Lime Works, trucking limestone that was used on farmers' fields. We eventually got into the sales business of trucks and cars, used cars and farm machinery. And we've been here since, here in Franklin County, St. Albans.

My ambition, after graduating from college, was to go to law school, stay in the army. Having gone to Norwich, I was commissioned. Then brother Floyd had kidney failure and Dad had a stroke, so I was home to operate the business until such time when they got well. Then [with] this peace in Korea at the time, they didn't need new fresh officers as much as they did earlier. So [there was] the opportunity to stay and work in the business with Floyd.

Politically, we were Democrat. I suppose the influence from Winooski made that decision for us. Father, much to everyone's amazement in Winooski certainly, was Republican. I think that's mostly because my mother grew up with Lee Emerson, who was one-time governor, in Barton, Vermont. But he'd come to Chittenden County. He'd always visit our house and stay. So I suppose his influence is the reason why my parents were Republican and not Democrat, even though they lived in Winooski. There weren't many Republicans in Winooski at the time.

I have not [been to Lebanon], but my father went back [during] Suez [in] 1956 with his brother to help rebuild the church that burned down. They conducted fund drives here among the family and raised some money to rebuild the church back in Lebanon. And they went back to see to it that it was done. We'd like to go but you're always nervous about how safe it is.

*Larry and Floyd Handy own three automobile dealerships in St. Albans. Floyd Handy served as mayor. Larry Handy served on the boards of Kerbs Memorial and St. Albans hospitals, and, after their merger, at Northwest Medical Center. He has been a Missisquoi Valley High School director, Vermont Automobile Dealers Association president, Vermont National Guard company commander, Franklin County Democratic Party co-chair and Vermont Public Service Board member.*

# Memories
# and Proverbs

# Memories of Winooski
## *by Clarke A. Gravel*

I well remember the Great Flood of November 3-5, 1927 when at the age of eleven, I stood on the Burlington side of the river near the current "Salmon Hole" and watched raging waters go by with all sorts of floating debris. The afternoon of November 4, the metal bridge between Winooski and Burlington went out with a horrendous noise. The gristmill, which stood at the intersection of First Street (now Riverside Avenue) and Colchester Avenue, was then blasted in order to allow clearer passage for the water. About a week later, a pontoon bridge was constructed and traffic was able to cross the river. Thereafter, on or about December 1, the water rose once again and the pontoon bridge went out.

When the pontoon bridge was reinstalled, I and another Burlington youngster rode atop a truckload of illegal alcohol, covered by a tarpaulin, which crossed on the pontoon bridge and delivery was made somewhere in Winooski. I vividly recall that the truck passed the then chief of police, Charles A. Barber.

Some years later, when I was a student at St. Michael's College, I worked a couple of Christmas holidays for Elias Desautels in the Champlain Mill doing inventory, and two summers in the

The Champlain Mill during the 1927 Flood. *(Courtesy of Clarke Gravel)*

woolen mill, one time in the weaving area and another time in the dressing area. Since I was related to one of the foremen in the American Woolen Mill (my brother-in-law, George E. Finnegan), I was assigned the worst job each time in order not to be given preference. At that time, I weighed 117 pounds and the metal box loaded with bobbins, which I carried to the weavers from a large bin, weighed approximately 100 pounds. When I worked in the weaving area, my job was to get down under the looms when they were stopped in order to clean out the lint and other material. I can assure you that the roaches inhabiting the same space appeared to be at least two inches long.

While a student at St. Michael's College, I hitchhiked from my home in the north end of Burlington to the college and, especially in the wintertime, stopped at Gabbeit's Diner [Bill's Diner] just around the corner from Main Street on East Allen Street in Winooski for coffee and warmth. I occasionally got my hair cut by Mr. Granger in his barber shop right on that corner. The only time you did not successfully reach the college or return by hitchhiking was on those bitter cold winter days when you had to walk.

Later in 1942, just a few months after graduating from law school, when Chittenden County elected a complete slate of Republicans, I was swept into office as the youngest state's attorney in the United States. I took over on December 21, 1942, when my predecessor resigned. My very first major case began shortly thereafter when, on January 3, 1943, an unknown man was found slain in Winooski. The victim had been stabbed repeatedly.

The body had been found lying on his back on a stone stairway leading from East Allen Street to the rear of what was then known as the "Bailey Block," which housed the Lavigne Funeral Parlour. During the investigation, which lasted at least two weeks, I became quite well acquainted with the same Charles A. Barber, the police chief, and we became fishing buddies. Efforts to identify the victim took an inordinate length of time, even though there were four "positive" identifications of the body, including two by ladies who believed themselves to be the widow of the victim. The victim was eventually identified as an itinerant and Leo L. Brown was determined to be the murderer. Brown was committed to the State Hospital for the insane and has since deceased.

My service as State's Attorney was during the World War II years when approximately five thousand soldiers were stationed at Fort Ethan Allen. Winooski knew the extent of their celebration on the weekend of each monthly payday when every area police department and the military police had to be brought together to maintain the peace. During that time, I issued a search warrant and accompanied a large number of these officers to raid the hotel then known as the "Franklin House," which was on lower Main Street, right near the abutment to the original bridge just north of the Champlain Mill. The hotel was later moved to East Canal

Street and still later it was demolished to make way for the current parking area.

The Franklin Hotel elevated on timbers for moving. Movers were Frank F. Russell and his sons, Harry and George. *(Courtesy of John and Joyce Mulhall)*

The raid resulted in rounding up about two hundred Winooski people, including a few of its leading citizens, all of whom were partaking of alcohol after hours. Chief Barber marched every single one of them up Main Street to the old police station on West Allen Street and required them to pass by a desk where he would occasionally fail to ask for a name but would state politely, "So, you're John Smith, are you not?" and carefully record that data. There were easily twenty or thirty Smiths and numerous Jones.

I served as State's Attorney until 1947, and was then elected Judge of Probate for Chittenden County. In that capacity, I had the pleasant opportunity to handle many matters such as adoptions, involving the citizens of this active community.

Another pleasant memory of Winooski involves my service as Assistant Clerk of the House of Representatives when Russell Niquette was a senator and Thomas Finnegan was Winooski's representative. Tom and I would await Senator Niquette's arrival, get into his automobile and race off to Essex where we would pick up another senator and head on down Route 2 to Montpelier, a journey which was perilous indeed during February and March (more perilous because Niquette had the habit of turning

*Vote for*
**CLARKE A. GRAVEL**

*for* **JUDGE OF PROBATE**

Poster for Atty. Gravel's first campaign for judge of probate in October 1946. He succeeded Francis Foley. *(Courtesy of Clarke Gravel)*

around, while driving, to talk to those in the rear seat).

One of the Finnegan cousins had married a gentleman named Wright and I remember quite well visiting the Finnegans in Winooski when I was in high school. I was fortunate enough to be drafted to accompany her to the [county] fair at Essex and, in later years, to proudly point out that I had dated Theresa Wright, a movie star!

*Clarke A. Gravel, a graduate of Saint Michael's College and Boston College Law School, formed the law firm Gravel and Shea in 1955, after serving six years as State's Attorney and eight years as Judge of Probate. He has been admitted to the Vermont Supreme Court and United States Supreme Court. He served as president of the Vermont Bar Association, and as chair and member of numerous judicial committees. He has also been past president of United Way of Chittenden County and participated in several community service organizations.*

## Murder in the Gristmill and Other Memories
### *Recollections of Laura Deforge*

I was born January 19, 1920 and grew up in Winooski Park across from Saint Michael's College. My mother was born in Bakersfield [Vermont]. They used to live in Bakersfield, my mother's parents. Course there wasn't any work so they come to the city to work. I think my grandfather must have lived in Burlington.

I was brought up around St. Michael's there. I lived near the limekiln in one of the company houses right in the middle of limekiln hill. My father worked at the limekiln. They used to burn four-foot cordwood in the kiln, like big ovens. My father used to load the wood into the firebox. And I can tell you that was a hot job to cook the stone. After the lime was cooked, they used to sort it. The best grade they sent to Maine to the paper companies to bleach the paper. We used to hear them holler when they were going to blast. Then the stones used to fly right through our windows.

I used to put lime in a pail [of water]. It would dissolve as soon as it hit the water; it would boil. It was almost like paste; it was almost like paint. And I'd whitewash the chicken coop; sometimes I'd use an old broom.

The limekiln never run steady all the time. My father was out of work quite a lot; he had to find other menial jobs; we were very poor. So that's how come my father's buried in the same plot as his mother because my mother didn't have any money to buy a new plot.

The little one-room

Burlington Flouring Mill, Winooski Falls c.1890. *(Courtesy of Special Collections, University of Vermont Libraries)*

schoolhouse, Ethan Allen School, between Fanny Allen Hospital and St. Mike's. I went there, graduated from the eighth grade there. Then I went to high school in Winooski. We used to have to walk, no matter if it was thirty degrees below zero, 'cuz we had no other transportation there.

The limekiln road crossed the Winooski River and the bridge built in 1914 that replaced the covered bridge. The flood of 1927 damaged the bridge, so they closed it. You couldn't even walk over it. The children who lived on the South Burlington side of the bridge couldn't get to the Ethan Allen School anymore. They couldn't go to school at all, 'cuz that was their school.

When I was growing up my mother told me my grandfather worked at the gristmill in Winooski [Falls], and that he was murdered there, that he was a card shark. She always believed that he got caught cheating, so some of the men threw him in the wheel pit.

On the other side, another member of the family, a relation, her mother told her that during his lunch hour he took a nap and he was sleeping on the belt, on the conveyor belt, and that when it was time to go to work, he hadn't awoken. They started up the belt and he went into the wheel pit. But I think they just wanted to keep the skeleton in the closet.

My mother never tried to hide the facts that he was murdered. My mother told that story to me and my sister when we were growing up. I've heard it many, many times. He is buried in Green Mountain Cemetery, but there's no inscription on the monument that says that he died at the gristmill. His name is Edmund Payne. He was my mother's father. My mother never hid the facts from us.

When he died, [my mother] was quite young. She had two sisters and a brother. Her brother was much younger. My mother went to work and looked after him and gave him an education. He finally settled in Rutland. He was a telegrapher on the railroad.

My grandmother died of, well they called it consumption back then. She used to work in the cotton mill down at Lakeside, where General Electric was. That used to be a cotton mill way back when. She died before my grandfather. And that's about all I can tell you.

# "First Come, First Served":
## Proverbial Wisdom from the World
## of the Millers and the Mills
### *by Wolfgang Mieder*

Proverbs from all nations contain much wisdom based on trades and occupations, and the venerable profession of milling is no exception. Mills driven by water were in use during classical antiquity, and windmills have been recorded since the very early Middle Ages. They clearly occupied a central role in mercantile life for centuries, and due to their common appearance in villages and cities, the folk began to generalize their observations and experiences relating to millers and their mills into colorful metaphors. There exist literally dozens of such proverbs, proverbial expressions, and proverbial comparisons based on the milling trade in many languages and cultures. Even though some of them date back to ancient times and even though the traditional life of millers and mills has been replaced by modern machines, much of the proverbial wisdom remains in common use today. People use this old formulaic language without necessarily understanding the precise meaning of the metaphors dealing with the vanished water- or wind-driven mills and their traditional millers. The old phrases have become linguistic relics of sorts, and while many have indeed gone out of use, there are those which hang on and which people of the modern age would not want to miss.

Take for example that ever present elliptic proverb "First come, first served," which certainly is one of the most popular proverbs today. But this somewhat colorless piece of wisdom actually had its origin in the world of milling, as can be seen from Geoffrey Chaucer's longer version in his *The Wife of Bath's Prologue* (c. 1386): "Whoso that first to mille comth, first grynt." About one hundred years later the *Paston Letters* (c. 1475) contain the reference "For who comyth fyrst to the mylle, fyrst must grynd." And yet another hundred years later Henry Porter in his *Two Angry Women of Abington* (1599) already cites the truncated version "So, first come, first seru'd." For the next three centuries the longer version referring to grinding at the mill continued to compete with the shorter more general rule. Both of them expressed the legal concept that whoever arrived first has the right to be taken care of first. But with mills disappearing from the landscape, the longer proverb variant has vanished from general parlance, and hardly anybody is aware anymore that the proverb "First come, first served" is in fact a legal proverb based on the customary law of grinding that person's grain first who is first in line at the mill. And it should be noted that this mill law is common throughout the European languages. The fact that Erasmus of Rotterdam cited it in Latin as "Qui primus venerit, primus motel" in his *Adagia* (1500ff.) helped to spread it from language to language through the process of loan translations.

But while this proverb is very much in use today, there is a second early English proverb to be found in the prologue of Chaucer's *Canterbury Tales* (c.1386) that has disappeared and is incomprehensible without any historical and cultural explanation: "Wel coude he stelen corn and tollen thries, / And yet he hadde a thombe of gold." The "tollen thries" refers to the miller who takes his toll three times, and the "thombe of gold" is an old jibe directed against a merchant keeping his thumb on the scales when weighing something. The actual proverb is the ironic "An honest miller has a thumb of gold," meaning that millers always cheat.

And steadily the millstone hums Down in the willowy vale.

From William Cullen Bryant's *The Song of the Sower,* 1881.

Perhaps the seventeenth-century proverb "The miller never got better moulter [toll] than he took with his own hands" with the meaning of knowing how to help oneself is a bit more positive, but it seems to allude at taking advantage of a situation as well. That certainly is the case with the proverb "The meal came home short from the miller" as an expression of disappointed expectations. Whether the expectations were justified or not, many a farmer would have felt cheated by the miller when confronted by the small amount of ground flour from the large quantity of grain originally supplied.

Such stereotypical expressions exist about other professions as well, notably against lawyers, physicians, and priests. But the invectives against millers are quite numerous, perhaps because farmers who brought their grain to the gristmill simply felt at the mercy of the miller's (dis)honesty in providing them with the meal due them. Such proverbs as "Put a miller, a weaver, and a tailor in a bag and shake them, the first that comes out will be a thief," "A miller is a thief," "Many a miller, many a thief," "Every miller draws water to his own mill," "Millers are the last to die of famine," "A miller is never dry" (is often intoxicated), and "The miller's pigs are fat, but God knows whose meal they ate" all reflect the questionable character of the miller in the eyes of those who are dependent on him. But then there is also the sixteenth century proverb that states that "Much water goes by the mill that the miller knows not of" which William Shakespeare cited as "More water glideth by the mill / Than wots the miller of" (*Titus Andronicus*, II,1,85). This is not necessarily directed negatively against the miller. The proverb simply states that one cannot pay attention to everything. Clearly the proverb "The miller grinds more men's corn than one" is a positive statement that comments on his involvement and experience with many parties, stressing that any particular person is not the only one to be considered. And the somewhat odd but still heard expressions "To put out the miller's eye" or "To drown the miller" are also not vicious attempts to harm a dishonest miller. They are nothing but innocuous metaphorical phrases referring to someone having added too much water to a recipe, especially one thickened with flour. A plausible explanation of the origin of the first expression states that "miller's eye" refers to lumps of flour not fully mixed into the batter. In certain recipes such lumps are desirable, but adding too much water can eliminate them, that is putting the miller's eyes out. The second expression with the same meaning simply alludes to the fact that millers using water wheels for power had little need for more water.

There are also a few proverbial comparisons that include references to the miller or mill which, while they were popular since the sixteenth century, have now become more or less obsolete: "No bigger than a miller's thumb" (a mere trifle), "Like a miller's mare" (awkward, clumsy), "Plump as a miller's sparrow" (well-fed), "Like a horse in a mill" (to walk around blindly), "As safe as a thief (mouse) in a mill" (very safe), "To be like a mill without a sluice" (talkative), and "To clack (clap) like a mill" (talkative). With mills barely to be seen today, such verbal images are prone to disappear from the language.

And proverbs about the mill itself? The proverb "The mill cannot grind with the water that is past" with its earliest citation from 1616 is still well-known today and refers to missed opportunities. But the 15th century proverb "A mill that grinds not is worth as much as an oven that bakes not" is not known anymore. Yet texts like "Enter the mill and you come out floury" and its longer variant "If you don't want flour on your happern [happin], you should keep out of the mill" as well as "Mills won't grind if you give them no water," "Still waters turn no mills," "Too much water drowned the miller," and "No mill, no meal" have all been recorded in use during the twentieth century in the United States. Somewhat related to the last text are the proverbs "The mill gets (gains) by going" and "The mill stands that wants [lacks] water," meaning only an operating mill will get things done. This proverb seems almost simplistic in its wisdom. The same is true for the proverb "A little stream drives a light mill" if one takes it only literally. In its metaphorical meaning the proverb alludes to the general truth that small causes will have small effects. Of interest is also the proverb "The mill that is always going grinds coarse and fine" since it was recorded for the first time only in 1910. In this case the "mill" is a euphemism for a person's mouth, hence the meaning that someone who talks too much cannot escape saying things now and then that would be better left unsaid. Talking of loquaciousness, it might be of interest to note that the mill was also a place where news was exchanged while one waited to have one's grain ground. Thus there exists the expression "Mill news" as well as the proverbs "If you will learn news, you must go to the oven [bakery] or the mill" and "A country-side smithy, a parish mill, and a public house - the three best places for news." And there is also the misogynous proverb that "Mills and wives are ever wanting." The addition of "It requires much to keep a mill useful, a wife fine" helps to explain the meaning of the proverb.

And, of course, there is the ever popular proverb "The mill(s) of God grind(s) slowly," which in its classical Greek and Latin form was "The mills of the gods grind slowly, but they grind small." There is also a small poem by the German poet Friedrich von Logau called "Retribution" (1654) which Henry Wadsworth

Longfellow in 1870 rendered into English as follows:

> Though the mills of God grind slowly,
> yet they grind exceeding small;
> Though with patience He stands
> waiting, with exactness grinds he all.

Thus retribution may be delayed, but it is certain to overtake the wicked sinners. Here we have God (or the ancient gods) as the ultimate miller metaphorically grinding up his imperfect children, that is, punishing them for their sins. The religious basis of this punitive proverb has been lost in modern times. In fact, often "God" is simply replaced by the secularized notion of "justice" or such banal terms as bureaucracy, administration, government, etc.

Of much interest also are the proverbial expressions based on the mill. Some expressions disappeared from active use some time ago. The phrase "To be born in a mill" was current in the sixteenth century and was employed to describe a person who spoke loudly (to overcome the noise in a mill; also a reference to deafness). The expressions "To go (pass) through the mill" and "To put someone through the mill" in the meaning of to undergo or subject someone to a hard, painful experience, training, or test are very much current today, even though people might not be thinking of actually being ground up between two millstones. The phrase that "Someone's mill has ground its last grist" in the meaning of being near to death has also been forgotten since the fifteenth century. But speaking of grist, there is the proverbial expression "To be (bring) grist to one's mill" which has maintained its currency since the sixteenth century. From the same time people also still use the phrase "To draw water to one's mill" with a somewhat similar meaning. Both proverbial expressions refer to an advantageous situation, with the former resulting in an advantage by chance and the latter helping that advantage along a bit. Yet the sixteenth century phrase "To bring more sacks to the mill" with the meaning of supplementing argument with argument or weight with weight appears to have fallen out of favor during the nineteenth century.

Speaking of weight, heavy millstones have also been the source of metaphorical expressions. There is the general proverb that "The lower millstone grinds as well (much) as the upper (higher)"

Burlington Flouring Mill Company, 1905. *(Courtesy of Vermont Historical Society, Charles G. Nash Gift, 1954)*

which comments on the fact that often two things or people must work together to be effective. Of little use today is the phrase "To see as far into a millstone as another man" that used to be employed as an ironic claim to acuteness. The phrase "To look through a millstone" is obviously related to this idea, once again referring to someone being very sharp sighted. Also lost is the absurd expression "To weep millstones" with the meaning of not likely to weep at all that was a popular term of Shakespeare's, as for example in "He will weep. - Ay, millstones, as he lessened us to weep" (*Richard III*, I,iii,353). And the seventeenth century proverbial exaggeration "To rain millstones" has been completely replaced by "To rain cats and dogs." Yet another exaggeration "To trust someone no further than one can fling a millstone" from the same time also appears to be out of common use.

Regarding proverbial comparisons, the appropriate images of "To weigh heavier than a millstone" and "Harder than (as hard as) the nether millstone" have long been favorites, and people still use the phrase "To be between the upper and nether millstones" to describe an inextricably difficult position as an alternate to such more frequent expressions as "To be between the devil and the blue (deep) sea" or "To be between a rock and a hard place." The same is true for "To sink like a millstone" with its clear allusion to the heaviness of this special stone. And then there is, of course, the well-known proverbial expression "To lay a millstone on someone's neck" and its variants "To be (carry) a millstone around one's neck" to refer to an especially heavy burden. The metaphor is based on a Biblical passage in which Jesus warns those who would dare to corrupt children: "But whoso shall offend one of these little ones which believe in me, it were better for him that a millstone were hanged about his neck, and that he were drowned in the depth of the sea" (Matthew 18:6). One is reminded of a more general interpretation of this fateful phrase in D.H. Lawrence's essay on "Democracy" (1917, published 1936): "Every individual is born with a millstone of ideals around his neck, and, whether he knows it or not, either spends his time trying to get his neck free or else he spends his days decorating his millstone." This is reminiscent of the proverbial comparison "To be like corn under a millstone" that refers metaphorically to life's often grievous oppression. And for individuals between millstones or with millstones around their neck, it is only natural to wish that their lives could at times be "As calm (placid, smooth, still) as a millpond" without the noise of the ever turning water wheel of that grist mill of life.

What are the chances of survival of the proverbial language cited as examples in this short survey of metaphorical wisdom relating to millers and mills? Some of them have already dropped out of general use, and their old and antiquated metaphors are in need of historical and cultural explanation in order to be understood at all. But there are also those more common expressions which will definitely continue to be effective images for modern life that is becoming ever more void of traditional mills. The stereotypical expressions relating to the miller are well to have disappeared, but people certainly will continue to struggle with millstones around their necks, and they will insist that the millers of the future will heed the old mill proverb "First come, first served." Nobody would want to miss that basic wisdom of fair social behavior.

*Dr. Wolfgang Mieder is chair of the German and Russian Department and a professor of German and folklore at the University of Vermont. He is also an internationally-known proverb scholar who has published numerous books on proverbs and proverbial expressions in German and in English.*

# At Work in the Mill

# Mill Photographers
## *by Jeffrey D. Marshall*

The advent of large textile mills on the banks of New England's rivers signified a fundamental change in the way people viewed and interacted with their workplace environments. The new mills with their power looms were objects of awe and pride, massive in size, noisier than almost any other workplace and amazingly productive. They represented a new force in the economy and a wholly new work style for those who found employment as textile workers. For these reasons, textile mills were natural subjects for the photographer's lens.

The first large mill at Winooski Falls was built in 1837 and employed 450 workers by the 1850s.[1] This coincided with the invention of photography in 1839 and its rapid development in the following decades. The first photographs were daguerreotypes, reverse images on polished metal plates. Daguerreotype photography required the subject to remain immobile for several seconds while the plate was exposed. Even though this requirement would seem to favor immobile objects rather than portraits, the process was used primarily for portraiture, and daguerreotype landscapes are relatively rare.

New processes appeared in the 1850s, and paper prints rapidly gained favor. By the early 1860s a distinctly new medium had evolved for landscape depiction: the stereograph. The stereograph featured two photographs, mounted on a card, taken at slightly different angles, producing a three-dimensional effect when viewed through a simple hand-held viewer. Three-dimensional images were especially effective when they encompassed a wide view with objects of varying depth. Thus, mountain scenery, natural wonders, bridges and buildings were popular subjects for the stereographer. Although they were designed primarily for entertainment, stereographs achieved something far more important: they established a broad photographic record of architecture and landscape that otherwise would have been lost to history.

Nineteenth-century landscape artists generally preferred grand vistas of natural beauty rather than pastoral or industrial scenery. Photographers such as William Henry Jackson and Carleton E. Watkins followed in the artistic tradition of the Hudson School of landscape painters, depicting the landscape of the American West as grand, beautiful, and virtually untouched by humanity.[2]

City scenery, or cityscapes, evoked very different ideals, such as civic pride, a sense of triumph over nature, and the desire to place oneself in a visual context. The perfect medium for this sort of image was the

Mill #1, Winooski c. late 1860s. *(Stereograph by A.F. Styles, courtesy of Special Collections, University of Vermont Libraries)*

picture postcard, which gained instant popularity after postal reforms allowed their use early in the 1890s. Printers flooded the market with postcards of scenes in nearly every city and village. The countryside and views of natural wonders continued to be popular in this new format, but town and city views were increasingly popular. Postcards appealed to tourists, who could document their travels and scribble messages home cheaply and efficiently.

Postcard views of Winooski tend to focus on the falls, and thus there are many good images of the textile mills from the 1890s on. These views can be dated, more or less, by the presence or absence of certain structures. The six-story Burlington Woolen Mill appears in the 1890s much as it did in 1860s, but by the 1890s more buildings have been added. The Colchester Merino Mill was constructed in 1880, perpendicular to the Burlington Woolen Mill. Another structure that we now call "the Woolen Mill" was added late in the 1890s. It was attached to the Colchester Mill and ran westward, parallel to the Burlington Mill. Further upstream, the Champlain Mill was built in 1912.[3]

Postcards usually portrayed mills and other working places in the context of the physical environment, the town or city of which it was a part. A very different format for these workplace portraits became popular in the early twentieth century. The panoramic photograph gave a very wide-angled view, allowing the photographer to cover a lot more territory and provide a whole different context.

In Burlington, Louis L. McAllister mastered the art of the panorama, using a camera with a lens that swivelled 180 degrees. Born in Omaha, Nebraska in 1876, McAllister moved to Vermont and began taking pictures in 1897. He purchased a panorama camera in 1915, and took his first panorama that year in Burlington's City Hall Park. His forte was the portrait, both in the panorama and the more traditional print sizes. McAllister considered himself a photographic purist. His photographs, particularly his panoramas, showed innovation, but he stuck to the old-style cameras and developed his own pictures in a simple, cluttered darkroom in his basement.[4]

McAllister called himself a photo-artist, but he probably would not have felt comfortable in the company of the great art photographer Alfred Steiglitz and the artists who named their movement the "photo secession," to distinguish their work from the more pedestrian uses of photography. McAllister clearly enjoyed taking pictures for hire, and he strove to make them as good as any portrait painter would. His work encompassed much more than portraits. For instance, he took pictures of road construction for the Burlington Street Department from the 1910s to the 1930s, creating a wonderful archive of Burlington street scenes when elm trees still arched over the streets.[5]

Segment of a Panorama of the Winooski Falls Mill Complex c.1920. *(By Louis McAllister, courtesy of Special Collections, University of Vermont Libraries)*

Because his equipment was bulky and heavy, McAllister took pictures that were carefully posed and often quite formal. Even the street scenes have a quality of formality to them. But they worked, because McAllister was meticulous in the technical aspects of his work, and because he had the artist's sense of what his camera was seeing.

The panorama puts the factory in a very different context from the postcard. It also allows for a different subject focus. Most of McAllister's panoramas are group portraits. McAllister created urban landscapes that, unlike earlier efforts, focused on the people who lived and worked in urban areas. Thus, the mills are portrayed not simply as buildings in an urban landscape but as places where people worked and from which they drew their identities. Nevertheless, neither the landscape pictures nor group portraits reveal very much about the work and lives of the people in the mills.

The mills brought jobs and a certain amount of prosperity to Winooski and other cities in the Northeast, but there was a dark side to this prosperity. For the mill workers, the hours were long and some of the work was dangerous. One of the worst abuses of the factories well into the twentieth century was the employment of child laborers. Children were hired for low wages and long hours to do much of the tedious, and sometimes dangerous work of tending the looms. Child labor was documented in Vermont by one of the most famous of the social-documentary photographers, Lewis Hine.

Born in Oshkosh, Wisconsin in 1874, Lewis Wickes Hine worked as a laborer until the age of twenty-five, when he entered teacher's school. In 1901 he was offered a job as a teacher in the progressive Ethical Culture School of New York City. Here, in 1904, he first began taking pictures of school activities. His photographs proved very popular. Hine's mentor and supervisor, Frank Manny, suggested that he take his camera to Ellis Island to document the multitudes of immigrants starting new lives in America. Hine followed the suggestion and produced a series of striking photographs of immigrants from all corners of Europe. He also photographed the recent arrivals in their New York tenement homes. In the process, though, he became aware of the horrible living and working conditions that many immigrants were forced to accept.[6]

Hine quickly became well-known for his photographs of urban destitution, showing a world that America's social establishment preferred to ignore. The progressive reform era was underway, however, and reformers were riding a wave of public concern about dangerous working conditions, unsafe

Louis McAllister in his Workroom c. 1945. *(By James Detore, courtesy of Special Collections, University of Vermont Libraries)*

housing, and hundreds of other abuses that affected working people. It was child labor that Hine adopted for his cause. In 1908 he accepted a job as photographer for the National Child Labor Committee. His photos would be used in pamphlets, reports, exhibits and press releases to raise public awareness of the abusive employment of children. As photographer for the National Child Labor Committee, Hine traveled around the country, sometimes risking bodily harm to gain entry into the factories. He would pose as a bible salesman, a fire inspector, a postcard salesman, or sometimes as an industrial photographer who had arrived to take pictures of machinery. Sometimes, he couldn't get in, so he settled for pictures of child laborers outside of the workplace.[7]

Vermont had a child labor law as early as 1867. Act 35 of the laws of 1867 outlawed the employment of children under ten "in any manufacturing or mechanical establishment." Children from ten to fifteen could work no more than ten hours a day in such an establishment. And no child under fourteen could work "in any mill or factory" unless he or she attended public school for at least three months in the year.[8]

The law was clearly inadequate in the new age of industrialism. For one thing, it exempted agricultural labor, which in some respects was worse than factory work. It didn't define what a manufacturing or mechanical establishment was. Children could still be employed in quarries, the lumber industry, retail establishments, and as piece-workers at home. The biggest loophole, however, was that there was no effective enforcement. There were no labor inspectors. The only officials who had any clear responsibility under Vermont law for child laborers were truant officers, who faced a difficult task trying to prove that a child hadn't attended school for three months in any particular year. In 1892 the required attendance at school was lengthened from three months to twenty-six weeks, and in 1894 to twenty-eight weeks. Also, the employment of children who couldn't read or write but were "capable of receiving such instruction" was forbidden.[9]

Clearly, the main concern of Vermont legislators in this pre-progressive era of the late nineteenth century was that children should have the opportunity to go to school. Some people surely believed that children whose parents allowed them to work in a factory probably would not prosper in school anyway; it was better to keep them employed than to give them the opportunity to make mischief. And then there were the children who apparently were not capable of literacy. This category might include children who had what we now call learning disabilities. It might also include recent immigrants who were literate in their native languages but were conveniently illiterate in English. There were, as well, the cases of children who had to work to support their families, because of the death or disability of a parent. Without workman's compensation, social security or disability insurance, the common laborer sometimes had to rely on the children to support the family.

Albert LaValle at American Woolen Company, Winooski c. 1910. Hine would take photographs outdoors when mill officials would not let him inside. (By Lewis Hine, courtesy of Robert Hull Fleming Museum, University of Vermont, gift of Daniel K. Mayers)

Later in his career, Hine changed the focus of his work. Rather than photographing laborers in the context of their harsh lives, he began taking pictures that emphasized the skills, the pride and dignity of their working lives. Some deplored this shift of focus, seeing it as a validation of the oppression of the workingman. But to Hine, the humanity of his subjects had always been the focus of his work, regardless of working conditions. Among the most famous of his later photos is a series of more than a thousand pictures that he took of the construction of the Empire State Building in the 1930s.[10]

Rose Wheel, twister at Winooski Mills c. 1943. *(By James Detore, courtesy of Special Collections, University of Vermont Libraries)*

Lewis Hine's later photographs resemble, in many respects, the work of a local photographer, James Detore. Born in Providence, Rhode Island in 1908, Detore moved to Winooski and attended the University of Vermont for three years, but because of the Great Depression was forced to drop out. While working as a bus driver, he opened a studio in the Old North End of Burlington in 1932. In 1941 he began a six-year career as photographer for the *Burlington Daily News*.[11]

It may have been this experience as a journalist that set Detore apart from his contemporaries, including Louis McAllister. His objective as a news photographer was not to take pictures that pleased people or that showed the world as they wished to see it, but to show things as they really were. This, of course, is exactly what Lewis Hine claimed to be doing with his child labor photographs. The truth is that no photographer is completely objective. If there is a purpose behind a picture, there is a bias behind it as well. Detore often took pictures as a news photographer that had a strong emotional bias, if not a quality of propaganda.

Outside of his journalistic work, Detore had a wide clientele, including many businesses such as the woolen mills. He took dozens of pictures in the Winooski mills. The subjects, mostly, are men and women at their workstations. Most of these pictures were taken in the 1940s when the demand for textile products was high, and employment in the Winooski mills had reached its peak.

The closing of the textile mills in the 1950s put the big mill buildings in a whole new context. Although new uses were found for most of the buildings, the sense of decline was evident. Some buildings fell into disrepair, or were partially boarded up. The mills were no longer the pride of Winooski, and to some they were eyesores. The urban landscape, once a scene of bustling activity, had become a post-industrial wasteland. But this view would not last long. By the 1970s, the federal Model Cities Program brought new life to the old mills. Most of Winooski's existing mills were restored and put to a variety of new uses. While very little of the renovated interior space suggested anything of the noise and activity of the mills, a sense of history pervaded the restored buildings.

The manner in which the textile mills were photographed tells a great deal about their place in the life of the community. The early stereographs and postcards depicted mill buildings as part of a scenic landscape, as noteworthy objects in the visual context of a riverside community. Lewis Hine added the human dimension of workers in the mills, with a strong suggestion that the workers – in this case, children – were victims of the mill. Louis McAllister's panoramas presented the mills in the form of a portrait, establishing a social context lacking in the older landscape photographs. McAllister's mill community suggests a far different perception of mill life than Hine put forth. James Detore's workplace photographs differed from the formal portraits of Louis McAllister, but shared in his view of the workers as a community of people who identified strongly with the place in which they worked. When the mills closed, the overriding perception of the mills once again became an external one, of objects now abandoned, or ill-used, in an urban landscape. The restoration of the mills, however, brought back a sense of usefulness and historical truth. While the mill community is no longer a part of the urban landscape in Winooski, the restoration of the buildings and the new purposes to which they have been adapted help to connect the mills and the people of Winooski to their past.

*Born and raised in Vermont, Jeffrey D. Marshall received a bachelor's degree in anthropology in 1978 and a master's degree in history in 1982 from the University of Vermont. He graduated from Simmons College with a master's degree in library science in 1988. He was a manuscript curator at the Massachusetts Historical Society; currently he is an archivist and curator of manuscripts at Special Collections, University of Vermont Libraries.*

## Mill Superintendent and Safety Director
### *Recollections of Raymond Roy*

*Raymond Roy was born in 1916 to Canadian immigrant parents. His father, Edward Roy, operated a creamery from 1911 until 1929, delivering milk to residents of Winooski and Burlington.*

*Raymond Roy has lived and worked in Winooski most of his life. When he was sixteen, he started at American Woolen Company mills as a part-time summer worker in the spooling department. In 1937, after high school and a year of business college, he returned to the mills where he worked in the efficiency department at $17.95 a week, before working his way quickly to management positions: superintendents' clerk, assistant superintendent, and superintendent of worsteds in charge of twenty-seven departments. (Worsteds are fine, smooth wool fabrics.)*

Raymond Roy, 1999. *(Courtesy of the Roy family)*

*He met his wife, Noelia LaMothe, at the mill. She worked as an inspector in the spooling department, checking threads for imperfections, earning $22 a week "which was really quite something [c. 1939]," Roy noted. After they were married, Mrs. Roy stayed at home to care for their two daughters and three sons.*

*Mr. Roy also worked briefly in Louisville, Kentucky for American Woolen, but returned to Winooski. When the Winooski mills closed in 1954, he became manager in charge of shutting down operations; then he spent a short time in St. Jerome, Quebec working for Regent Knitting Mills. Later, in Winooski, he was vice president at Lavallee & Roy, a machine tool company manufacturing precision instruments. His enthusiasm for his work and his interest in the complexity of textile manufacture carried over to his retirement; he continued to share his knowledge of mill operations with countless people until shortly before his death in June 2000.*

When I became the assistant superintendent, Mr. William Muir, who was the resident manager, called me one day and told me that now that we were on government work, we had to have a qualified safety director. That was required by the government. About 1940. So I took a course in industrial safety engineering at the University of Vermont. That was a long winter. [The course] started in September and it ended the last of April, two nights a week. Working full-time during the day and taking a course at night was really something. They [the mill] paid the tuition, for the books, the whole thing. I would work on weekends to cover [inspect for safety] all of the departments – the twenty-seven departments – once a month. And the pay was very good. I got time-and-a-half and that was great, because my standard pay was good to start with.

Whenever an accident took place that required medical attention, I'd be called in. I had charge of the First Aid. We had a nurse, a full-time registered nurse on first shift, and one on second shift. I'd be called in to inspect what happened and see what we could do to better the situation. Safety was always a concern from way back. In a textile plant, you've got an awful lot of gears, an awful lot of moving parts, and as a result, you had guards wherever you needed guards as much as possible.

Where you had one hundred spinning frames, your mode of transmitting power back then was a very efficient way – line shafts that used to go the whole length of the room, and they were belt-driven. The machines were all belt-driven. A spinning frame is forty-five feet long, and of course the mode of transmitting power was these belts. You had guards in case the belts would snap or

Colchester Merino Mills Spinning Room. *(From* Picturesque Burlington, *1894)*

break. There was quite a give in the belts, because the belts in the spinning department were seventy-two feet long. And if a belt would break, it would usually just drop. [There were] not too many [major accidents]. Fingers, stuff like that.

One time one fella darn near cut his whole hand off. After the healing, we sent him to Boston so that he could get the use of his hand back, not totally. Through the insurance this was all taken care of. We were never afraid of a fatality or anything like that. Once in a while [they lost arms] – that was way before my time. Remember one-arm Finnegan, one-arm Côté. Tom Finnegan, that was in the card room.

There were some that knew a lot more about these accidents. They'd seen many of 'em, arms you know. God, when I first saw it. It happened in our department, too. He was a fixer (repairman) on the winder. It was his fault in a sense. Carelessness. Whenever he worked on the big winder which was about thirty-five feet long, he was supposed to, when he stopped the motor, put a notice on where you throw the switch: DO NOT START THIS MACHINE. He had forgotten to put one on. It was during lunch hour and he had a little job to do. Instead of walking down to the length of the room for putting that red poster on the switch, he hadn't done it. A fellow came along, threw the darn switch on and [the fixer's] arm was caught between the frame of the winder and a big cam. That was the worst one.

But, you know, these were all machines. And oftentimes these people got to the point where they were immune to these machines, because you had to watch what you were doing and we had guards all over. They became immune to the machines; the machines were their friends. Like a saw, my saw would never cut my finger, you know. Well, when you get too comfortable, you forget. And at times that machine may get hungry. Carelessness usually would do that.

## An Interview: John O'Brien, Former General Manager
### Recollections of John O'Brien,
### recorded by Robert E. O'Brien, M.D.

John O'Brien's parents emigrated from County Roscommon, Ireland in 1890 and settled in Winooski. His father worked at American Woolen as a watchman. John was born in 1892. After his father died in 1906, he had to leave school to work in the mills to support his mother and four younger siblings. His siblings were able to finish high school; two of them went to college. Besides working at the mill, every weekend he would walk to Fort Ethan Allen to sell his mother's homemade "penny pies" to the soldiers. He started at the mills as an office boy when he was thirteen and worked up to general manager of a workforce that approached three thousand during World War II. He was a kind and generous man, highly respected by all the workers.

John O'Brien, Former General Manager, American Woolen Company mills, Winooski Falls. *(Courtesy of the O'Brien family)*

When he married Yvonne Provost, a French Canadian mill worker from Winooski, he could speak no French; she could speak no English. For years, he, his wife and their sons Thomas, John William and Robert, lived one block from the mill in a two-tenement house on the corner of West Allen and Weaver streets. When the Winooski mills closed, he became manager at American Woolen in Enfield, New Hampshire, then in Barnwell, South Carolina. After returning to Winooski, he served as city councilman for six years, and later as state representative for ten years.

In 1983, Winooski physician Robert E. O'Brien interviewed John O'Brien, his ninety-one-year-old father, about his experiences as general manager of American Woolen mills in Winooski:

*So you went to work [at American Woolen] in 1906?*

Yes I did. In those days the workweek was sixty hours a week – six days a week, ten hours a day, so that we could have Saturday afternoon off. At that time it was a great thing and people enjoyed it very much. [Employees might have worked some twelve-hour days to have Saturday afternoon off.]

*What was the pay scale in those days?*

The pay scale in those days was $8.25 for sixty hours a week and then it finally increased a little until it got up to about $15 a week, which was about seven years after I started to work there.

*Can you tell us about who was the manager of the mills. . . ?*

Well, the manager of the mill was George E. Whitney and he came here intending to buy the mills. He owned mills in Lebanon, New Hampshire and some of the people who worked in the old company here told him about the mill here and so he came up and looked it over with the intention of buying it. But, the owner of the American Woolen Company wouldn't sell. . . He wanted to keep it in the company, and he had started the Lawrence Woolen Company. He started it in Lawrence, Massachusetts and the Ayre Mill was the first mill that they owned there. Although, there were other mills there before that.

*What type of materials did they make?*

We made 100% wool; it wasn't all virgin wool but some percentage of it was, but it had to be of good quality.

*Did you make worsted material too?*

In about 1911 or 12, they started the Worsted Mill. The Mill was built on the east side of Main Street.

*That's the building that is called the Champlain Mill today; they redeveloped it.*

That's right. It's called the Champlain Mill; before that the Mills were called Burlington Mills. They built this new mill and had to go by the name Champlain Mill.

*Now do I understand that the worsted was made on the east side of Main Street and that the woolen was on the west side?*

At that time, yes. After 1912, worsted was on the east side of Main Street and the woolen was on the west side of Main Street. At about 1932, they [American Woolen] bought that mill across the river, known as the Chace Mill.

*That would be in Burlington, on the Burlington side of the river.*

Yes, on the Burlington side of the river and that was kept going until the mills shut down in 1945 [corrected by son – 1954].

*What about power? I understand that you could generate a lot of your own power from the Winooski Falls in the river?*

That's right. That is up until 1911 the power was generated by water power and in 1911 there was a turbine built and that would generate enough power to run the mills. If we had just a small crew working, we would shut down the regular power and run by the water. We employed normally around 1,900 people, between 1,800 people and 2,000 people. During the war (World War II), we employed 3,000 for three shifts.

*How about World War I? Did you make materials for the army in World War I?*

Yes we did. We made material for the army in World War I.

*How many people did you employ during World War I?*

During World War I, we employed probably around 1,800.

*I understand that during World Wars I and II, most of the GIs slept under American Woolen Company blankets and wore American Woolen Company clothing uniforms. Is that right?*

That's right. The blankets were made and we made the uniform blouses with all worsted. Very fine materials.

*I understand that after World War II, the American Woolen Company hit very bad days. Is that correct?*

Yes, they did.

*What seemed to be the major problems?*

In [those] days, they would have what they would call openings. They would start selling at fall and spring. They would call it the "ball and the swing." [American Woolen offices in New York would drum up sales for spring patterns and for fall patterns, which meant a letdown in production between seasons.] It got so that it wasn't working out too well and they finally decided to dispense with that and just have it year around instead of twice a year in New York. (Dr. O'Brien recalls that the "ball and swing" continued for a long time.)

*What effect did that have on your business?*

Well, it was better that way than it was before.

*But what happened to the mills. What was the basic reason that they finally moved south?*

Well, lower wages and no unions. Although we didn't have any trouble with the unions here but they seemed to think they would be better off if they were in the south where they didn't have any unions.

*What effect do you think the synthetic fabrics that were developed at that time had on the woolen business?*

Well, it didn't have too much effect on the woolen business because we had to incorporate some of this synthetic material. Probably 25% would be synthetic and 75% would be wool.

*It seemed that the heyday of the Woolen Company was during the war years when you were busy making clothing and blankets for the armed forces. What about the period of the Great Depression? That must have been a rough time for the woolen mills and the people of Winooski.*

It was very rough. The people were really up against it. We divided the work. If we had a husband and wife working, we had to decide which one would work and the other would have to be laid off. It was really a tough time.

*I understand that before the Depression, the Woolen Company owned a lot of property which they rented to employees, and that you sold out those properties at auction to the people of Winooski.*

Well, they hired a concern to come in here and auction off the different properties. They did it all in one day. They would come and stand before one house, and people would gather, and they would explain what the house was like, and they would take bids, and sell the property.

*So I would imagine that a lot of the property went for a very low price.*

Yes, some of it did. And some of it should have gone lower, but they had people to bid against the one that really wanted to buy the property. A couple of guys were paid to out-bid the ones that wanted it.

*I understand also that you had some part-time coaches at Winooski High School who really were employees of the Woolen Mill that you would release and pay them for coaching the high school ball team. Is that right?*

Yes, we did that. They didn't take much time off. Sometimes they didn't have to take any time off because it was generally late in the afternoon and it was pretty near closing time so we'd let them out.

*Mr. O'Brien, you mentioned that Mr. Whitney was the manager of the Woolen Mills when you started working there. When did his term end, and who were the succeeding managers?*

He retired in 1944 and he was succeeded by a man named William Muir. He stayed for two years and he went to Lawrence to another mill and I succeeded him and I worked as manager for about ten years.

*Thank you very much, Mr. O'Brien, for these interesting reminiscences.*

# Regulating Child Labor in Vermont
## by Paul Gillies

Sheep (and people) produce wool. The sheep just grazes. People have to shear it, card it, spin it, and weave it into something. Early Vermont families made their clothing and blankets this way, by hand. The effort filled the evenings with busy activity.

Small industry arrived in Vermont once the streams were developed for mills. With the invention of power carding, by 1810 there were 139 carding mills in Vermont producing 800,000 pounds of wool a year. In all parts of Vermont, 14,800 looms produced a million yards of wool cloth in that year.

The hills were cleared for raising sheep. By 1840, there were 1.6 million sheep in Vermont. The mills grew larger and more specialized. That year the state had 96 woolen mills and 236 fulling mills, together employing almost 1,500 workers.[1]

For the sheep industry, that was the best it ever was. From that time on, with the growth of railroads and changing regional economies, Vermont saw the end of sheep farming as a principal occupation of Vermont farmers. The cost of maintaining sheep in the West was a quarter of what it was in Vermont, and Vermonters began to reduce their herds, eating their sheep rather than harvesting the wool. By 1880, the hillsides were growing in again with bushes and trees, and hill farms were being abandoned. Dairy farming began to look like the answer.

The mills continued in operation, however, long after the agricultural side of the sheep industry had passed, importing the materials needed to make cloth. Vermonters learned the skills of operating machinery and working in the mills. There was plenty of waterpower to keep the machinery running. Mills in Winooski, Bridgewater and Bellows Falls, among others, were successful operations.

Mills were operated by people of all ages. Women and children were often employed in the mills, and as the end of the nineteenth century approached there was a growing concern for their welfare.

## 1. The Problem of Child Labor

All parents expected their children to help in the home. In an agricultural community, children were also needed in the fields and the barn. No Vermont law has even attempted to regulate child labor on the farm, except through mandatory education laws.

Children were to attend school. This was the law, from 1867 forward. Before that time, towns were required to maintain schools, but the keeping of schools was designed for times when children were not occupied with planting or harvesting crops.

In the villages, larger towns and cities, children went to work in the mills and factories with their parents from an early age. The family needed the extra income that the children provided, and economics settled the question of what to do with them during working hours. Workplaces were poorly designed; bad lighting, little ventilation and dangerous conditions threatened the health and lives of all workers, including children.

State government recognized the problem. The federal government recognized the problem. How these two governments succeeded in enacting comprehensive child labor laws is the story of governments coming to grips with their proper role. Today when the legislature sees a problem, it soon tries to enact a law to combat it. That was not always the view of the legislature. For much of the nineteenth century, especially in Vermont, business remained determinedly unregulated. There were no laws governing hours, wages or conditions. The business of government was promoting business, not regulating it.

Child labor laws have many purposes. The first and most important is the welfare of the child, protection from accidents and

"Carl Brown, eleven years old . . . He and his father run a farm of 160 acres in southern Vermont. He is overgrown, sluggish, but he said, "I'd rather go to school." *(By Lewis Hine c.1915, courtesy of Robert Hull Fleming Museum, University of Vermont, gift of Daniel K. Mayers)*

death, unhealthy occupations, long hours and low pay. The second is educational. School should come first. The more a child works, the less time he or she will spend in school.

Vermont was the first state in the union to abolish slavery,[2] but the employment of children with their parents' consent was an entirely private matter. The state would not interfere unless the subject became a public charge, as poverty placed the control of poor children in the hands of the local overseers of the poor.

Boys working in American Woolen Mill, Winooski c. 1910. These boys ranged in age from thirteen to fifteen. They had worked in the mill for one year or more; most were illiterate. *(By Lewis Hine, courtesy of Robert Hull Fleming Museum, University of Vermont, gift of Daniel K. Mayers)*

The development of child labor laws in Vermont is one aspect of the extraordinary change in society brought on during the national Progressive Era (1900-1917) and the equally important shift over the next two decades when Congress and the Supreme Court changed the face of federalism.

Vermont Progressives fought and won victories on many fronts, from election reform to labor laws, including the enactment of workmen's compensation, factory inspection, and laws protecting women in the labor force. The new federalism of the U.S. Supreme Court, following the depression of the 1930s, was a direct judicial response to the progressivism of the Congress and state legislatures a generation earlier. The fundamental question was which level of government would have primary authority over regulating child labor.

## 2. How Vermont Law Developed

The Vermont General Assembly first addressed the issue of child labor in 1837. It passed a law making selectmen and overseers of

Young Girls working in American Woolen Mill, Winooski, 1909. (*By Lewis Hine, courtesy of Robert Hull Fleming Museum, University of Vermont, gift of Daniel K. Mayers)*

the poor responsible for investigating the treatment of children working in mills and factories. The legislature wanted these officials to check to see if "the education, morals, health, food or clothing of such minor is unreasonably neglected, or that such minor is treated with improper severity or abuse, or is compelled to labor at unseasonable hours or times, or in an unreasonable manner."[3] If selectmen found such conditions, they were authorized to *admonish* the adults in charge of these children, and nothing more. Overseers of the poor might relocate the children of paupers to other places of employment.[4]

This act is evidence of an early public awareness of the problem of child labor in Vermont. The legislature must have concluded that a public admonishment was sufficient to expose a concern and stimulate attention to the problem. Enforcement was entirely local. No state official had authority over the way children were treated at work.

On November 15, 1867, the General Committee of the Vermont House reported its findings on a bill proposing maximum hours for child labor. The mill owners had testified their employees work from ten to fourteen hours per day, with twelve to thirteen hours the rule, that they had heard no complaints, and that no legislation was needed.

There was, however, one exceptional case presented – that of the

Winooski Woolen Factory, in the town of Colchester. It was stated that this factory employs from six to seven hundred hands. They work fourteen hours. That the operatives have asked repeatedly for shorter hours, and have been refused. That their pay is small, and that from seventy-five to one hundred of these are under twelve years of age.[5]

Colchester's town representative appeared before the committee in support of the bill he had sponsored, having been elected to the legislature on this issue. He had encouraged people in other towns to draft petitions in support of the legislation. He had furnished copies of petitions to members of the House, requesting their circulation. Child labor law was his issue.

The farmers in the legislature were worried; many felt that a general rule was not needed, that some special assistance should be given to Colchester, rather than making it a general enactment. The bill was then recommitted to the General Committee. Several days later, the bill re-emerged on to the House floor, with a startling announcement. The Colchester representative appeared to have misled the committee. F.C. Kennedy from the Winooski Woolen Mill appeared at a second hearing, along with five citizens of his town, and testified that five hundred persons worked at the mill, 35% male, 40% adult females, none under twelve and one-half years of age, and but two under thirteen. He said there had been no complaint by any worker that twelve hours of work a day was being overworked, for pay equal to that paid in Lawrence, Massachusetts. His operatives, he said, were generally healthy, and the mill was in a "flourishing condition." The member from Colchester later conceded that Mr. Kennedy's testimony was correct, that his own prior statements were hearsay. The General Committee announced that it was "now of opinion that no legislation is necessary upon the subject of the bill, and therefore recommend that it *ought not* to pass."[6]

But it did. Over the objections of the committee, the General Assembly adopted Vermont's first child labor and mandatory school attendance law. The act set ten years as the minimum age for manufacturing, and limited hours for children under the age of fifteen to no more than ten hours a day in a mill or factory. Constables, state's attorneys and town grand jurors were authorized to enforce the law, with a $50 penalty for violations.[7]

Another law enacted the same day prohibited the employment of children under fourteen in any mill or factory, "unless such child has already attended a public school three months within the year next preceding." It provided for a ten to twenty dollar fine for violating the law, to be paid by the parent, guardian, employer or overseer of the poor who allowed such employment. The town would enforce the law; one-half of the fine would go to the complainant, one-half to town of residence. Every child between the ages of eight and fourteen would attend three months of school a year, "unless such child has been otherwise furnished with the means of education for a like period of time, or has already acquired the branches of learning taught in the public schools."[8]

The 1867 legislation was not a unique Vermont phenomenon. Child labor laws affecting mill and factory work had become a national cause following the Civil War. Massachusetts and Connecticut had limited the workday of children under fourteen to ten hours as early as 1842. Vermont was the last state in New England to regulate child labor.[9] Southern states resisted the national movement.

Minimum schooling increased to twenty weeks in 1888, through a comprehensive revision of the state's education laws. That act made a stronger commitment to ensuring that all children attended school by adding a penalty for nonattendance. The fine was the amount on the grand list of a parent, guardian or master of the public money the school district would have spent on the student had he or she attended. The act also prohibited children in any labor under the age of fourteen who could not "read or write but [are] capable of receiving such instruction."[10] In 1894, this was increased to cover any child under fifteen years, and the school year was extended to twenty-six weeks. Truant officers were given the right to stop any child under fifteen and deliver him or her to school. Habitual offenders were sent to the state reform school for not less than twenty-six weeks.[11]

The organization of the Vermont Federation of Labor in 1903 in Barre was a stimulus for further legislation. As a result of its efforts and those of other support groups, the legislature increased the minimum age for work in the mills from ten to twelve in 1904.[12] That minimum age applied to any factory or workshop, or to carrying and delivering messages for a corporation or company as well. That year the legislature also added a new prohibition against employment of any person under sixteen, without a certificate from the school proving he or she had attended twenty-eight weeks of school during the year. A new restriction prevented those under fifteen working past 8:00 p.m.[13]

In the next session of the General Assembly, in 1906, the legislature required all children under sixteen to complete the full nine-year elementary school course in order to work in railroading, mining, manufacturing, quarrying or delivering messages for corporations or companies, except during vacations and before and after school, without a certificate from the school. The 8:00 p.m. curfew applied to anyone under sixteen.[14] Over the years, the occupations that were governed by this law increased. In 1910, for instance, the list included work in a hotel or bowling alley. That year the law also obliged parents to send their children between the ages of five and eighteen to school.[15]

The minimum age for mill work was increased in 1911. For work places with more than ten employees, the minimum was fourteen; for smaller mills, the minimum remained twelve. That year certain jobs were declared unfit for those under sixteen, including work involving sewing machine belts and the maintenance or cleaning of equipment. The law also required employers to provide chairs for girls under eighteen in jobs "where such employment compels them to remain standing constantly."[16]

The Vermont branch of the National Child Labor Committee was organized in Burlington in 1912, and began studying conditions in the mills. Their report highlighted the unhealthy working conditions and long hours of women and children. The Episcopal Diocese of Vermont conducted its own survey of conditions throughout the state. Its committee's report told of a fifteen-year-old child working more than thirteen hours a day for over a month who was fired for not reporting to work at 2:00 a.m. on a Sunday morning.[17]

The *Burlington Free Press* took up the charge, publishing a series of articles about conditions in the mills of Burlington and Winooski in 1912. A legislative committee, on a tour of the American Woolen Company mill in Winooski, found several pregnant women at work, one within ten days of delivery, and thirteen children under six years of age at the mill.[18]

As a direct result of the attention paid to the problems, new laws in 1913 set maximum hours for children working in manufacturing. The limit was eleven hours a day and fifty-eight hours a week for those under eighteen, nine hours and fifty hours for those under sixteen. The law also set a new minimum starting time of 7:00 a.m., while retaining the 8:00 p.m. curfew. The legislature also provided for the first state system of factory inspection that year.[19]

The 1917 law included an interesting provision, allowing an exception to the rules limiting the hours of work for children. Employing children contrary to the law of maximum hours was allowed if "such employment was to make up time lost on a previous day of the same week, in consequence of the stopping of machinery upon which such woman or child was employed or dependent for employment; but stopping of machinery for less than thirty consecutive minutes shall not justify employment at a time not stated in such notice."[20]

An exception to the child labor laws in 1919 allowed the commissioner to suspend the law in the case of a manufacturing establishment, when the products and materials were perishable and required immediate labor.[21]

In the minutes of the House Committee on Commerce and Labor for March 10, 1937, Mr. Olney, representing the Associated Industries in Vermont, vigorously opposed a proposal to reform

Jo Bedeon, a back-roper in the mule room, Chace Cotton Mill, Burlington, 1909. *(By Lewis Hine, courtesy of Robert Hull Fleming Museum, University of Vermont, gift of Daniel K. Mayers)*

the child labor laws introduced that year, saying it was "drastic, all-embracing, purposeless in that it seeks to legislate against conditions not existing in Vermont, not in keeping with the Vermont tradition and foreign to it." He testified there was no child labor problem in Vermont, explaining that employers don't employ child labor because they recognize the inefficiency of it. Vermont, he said, "was in a position today, because of favorable laws, to attract employers from other states who were being hampered by labor legislation. Vermont's labor history was attractive to out-of-state employers and should be kept attractive."

This antagonized at least one member of the committee. Mr. Rock cross-examined Mr. Olney and told him he "wanted no outside employers attracted to this state because our laws were less humane than those of other states." Rock asked Olney to inquire of his legal counsel if "it was not possible to work an eleven-year-old body twenty-four hours a day in this state under certain conditions, namely, not in prohibited very hazardous occupations, when the boy has completed 8 grade. He cited self as example of one who had done so at eleven."[22]

That year a reform bill passed the legislature. That act reduced the maximum hours for children under eighteen and women in mining, quarrying, manufacturing or mechanical work to no more than nine hours a day and fifty hours a week, and expanded the types of industries that could not employ children under sixteen. A new requirement in the certificate that it demonstrate the child is physically fit for work was added. The new law also required employers to keep records of all daily and weekly hours of women and children, and keep them open for inspection.[23]

In 1943, the legislature gave the commissioner the authority to suspend the law during times of emergency (but curiously not including the war as an emergency) to allow children sixteen to eighteen to work up to ten hours a day and sixty hours a week in certain industries.[24] Finally, in 1987, a new exception was added to the laws relating to maximum hours. Children working on motion pictures, in radio or television, would be excluded from the limits that applied to everyone else.[25]

### 3. How Federal Law Developed: The First Two Tries
With the support of the National Child Labor Committee, Congress enacted the Owen-Keating Act in 1916, prohibiting

interstate shipment of goods in commerce produced by children under the age of fourteen or those between fourteen and sixteen who worked more than eight hours a day or forty hours a week. Southern textile manufacturers brought a Commerce Clause challenge, claiming that the law went beyond the authority granted Congress by the Constitution, in *Hammer v. Dagenhart*. In a decision that surprised many constitutional scholars, the U.S. Supreme Court by a five to four vote found the new law unconstitutional in 1918.[26]

In 1898, the Supreme Court had ruled state maximum hour laws in hazardous jobs constitutional in a case approving a Utah law limiting miners and stone workers to eight hours a day.[27] In *Muller v. Oregon* (1908), the Court agreed that a state had the authority to set maximum hours for women.[28] What *states* could do, however, proved to be a different question from what the federal government could do.

The Supreme Court had already upheld federal law prohibiting the interstate sale of lottery tickets in 1911.[29] It had sustained the power of Congress to adopt the Pure Food and Drug Act and federal laws prohibiting the transportation of women across state lines for prostitution.[30] The Commerce Clause justified each of those acts. But child labor laws were different. They had the possibility of stopping all commerce, according to Justice William Day, writing for the majority. "The grant of power to Congress over the subject of interstate commerce was to enable it to regulate such commerce," he wrote, "and not to give it authority to control the States in their exercise of the police power over local trade and manufacture."[31]

The argument over states' rights had divided the nation many times in its history, with the South and Northeast frequently at odds over the proper role of the federal government in matters some regarded as purely local. "In interpreting the Constitution," wrote Justice Day, "it must never be forgotten that the Nation is made up of States to which are entrusted the powers of local government. And to them and to the people the powers not expressly delegated to the National Government are reserved."[32]

Justice Oliver Wendell Holmes's dissent is one of his most memorable: "I should have thought that if we were to introduce our own moral conceptions where, in my opinion, they do not belong," he wrote, "this was pre-eminently a case for upholding

Addie Laird in the North Pownal, Vermont, Cotton Mill, 1910. "She said she was twelve years old; others said she was really only ten." *(By Lewis Hine. Source: National Archives, Washington D.C.)*

the exercise of all of its powers by the United States."[33] He argued that all regulation means the prohibition of something. But he argued to a minority of the Court.

*Hammer v. Dagenhart* today stands as the high-water mark of a whole school of jurisprudence. That school believed government had no authority to interfere with business, that at best the states should have exclusive authority over the means of production. Conservative thinking like that was soon replaced with a new, more liberal approach to social problems, especially those relating to the way business was conducted. The spirit hit Congress and the Vermont legislature at about the same time. The courts were the last to change.

Not to be thwarted by the loss of *Hammer v. Dagenhart*, Congress passed a new child labor law the following year, having the same provisions regulating commerce, but instead of an outright prohibition, the new law provided a tax of ten percent on the profits of employers of child labor.[34] It had no greater success than the earlier law.

What defeated the second federal child labor law was an exception. If you didn't *know* a child was too young to work at your mill, you could not be held liable. To Chief Justice William Howard Taft, this feature revealed the true nature of the federal law. It was not a tax; it was a regulation against child labor, which was forbidden. That was the states' business. To allow a tax to justify intrusion of the federal government into such matters "would be to break down all constitutional limitation of the powers of Congress and completely wipe out the sovereignty of the states," he explained.[35]

The supporters of federal child labor laws were not discouraged. They tried another approach. If the Court could not find authority for child labor laws in the U.S. Constitution, then the Congress and the states would have to add language authorizing the regulation to the Constitution directly through an amendment.

### 4. A Constitutional Amendment on Child Labor

In 1924, Congress proposed a constitutional amendment to authorize national child labor laws. The proposal granted the federal government the authority to regulate child labor, but went on to promise that the power of the states was to remain unimpaired except where necessary to give effect to the laws enacted by Congress.[36]

When the Vermont General Assembly took up the question in the first months of 1925, there was near unanimous opposition to the amendment. The House voted 229 to 3 to support a resolution rejecting the amendment. The legislature concluded the proposal violated the Tenth Amendment to the U.S. Constitution and Article V of the Vermont Constitution. "Believing . . . that the proposed amendment would tend to invade and vitiate the rights of the State of Vermont," Vermont refused to ratify the amendment.

The *Burlington Free Press* editorial the day following the vote tried to explain the feeling of the legislature: "This does not mean that Vermonters are less interested in the welfare of children than are the people of any other State. It merely means that Vermonters feel they are able to regulate the labor of their children without help from Congress and it believes other states should be given the opportunity to do likewise." Vermont was telling Congress, "Hands off our internal affairs."[37]

Representatives from the Federal Council of Churches, General Federation of Women's Clubs, the League of Women Voters, and the Congress of Parents and Teachers were outraged by the vote. They believed southern textile companies were behind an announcement by the Farmers' States Right League that had an unfair impact on the outcome.[38]

In the end the amendment failed. Only twenty-eight states ratified it.[39] States' rights had been a rallying cry from the south prior to the Civil War. In Vermont, it was to become an article of faith as the new century progressed. George Aiken made a national reputation opposing the "federal boys" who sought to make a Vermont version of the Tennessee Valley Authority flood control projects in Windham County in the 1930s, and even enjoyed a brief flirtation with presidential aspirations as an opponent of FDR.[40]

Not that Vermont had reason to oppose the principles of federal child labor laws. It had already enacted laws with much the same force and effect, as early as 1867 but more recently in the spate of lawmaking that reached its crescendo in 1917. Vermont never saw the need for a constitutional amendment of its own.[41] It never wavered in its support of laws regulating child labor, but it was too independent to cede all lawmaking over important matters to the Congress.

### 5. Federal Regulation of Child Labor Validated

The third attempt to enact federal child labor laws also failed. Congress passed the National Industrial Recovery Act in 1933, which included hours and conditions for child labor. Two years later the act was declared unconstitutional by the Supreme Court as an unconstitutional delegation of power to the President. Child labor itself was not the principal target of the legislation or the decision.[42]

Finally, in 1938, Congress passed the Fair Labor Standards Act, which established the basic rules of child labor of federal law that remain in place today. This act prohibited employment of children under sixteen in certain occupations and under eighteen in designated hazardous occupations. It came under immediate attack, but this time the high court vindicated federal child labor laws in *United States v. Darby Lumber Co.* (1941).[43] *Darby* expressly overruled *Hammer v. Dagenhart.* Justice Harlan Stone wrote that in *Hammer*:

". . . it was held by a bare majority of the Court over the powerful and now classic dissent of Mr. Justice Holmes setting forth the fundamental issues involved, that Congress was without power to exclude the products of child labor from interstate commerce. The reasoning and conclusion of the Court's opinion there cannot be reconciled with the conclusion which we have reached, that the power of Congress under the Commerce Clause is plenary to exclude any article from interstate commerce subject only to the specific prohibitions of the Constitution."[44]

The *Darby* court saw *Hammer* as an anomaly. But this was also a different Court. President Roosevelt had changed the character of the Court through his appointments, and those justices ushered in a new and expanded role for the federal government in new areas of law, including the use of the Commerce Clause. At last a federal child labor law had passed constitutional review.

### 6. Present Law

a. State Law. Today, the Vermont law on child labor prohibits children under the age of fourteen from working in a mill or factory.[45] Minors over fourteen may work in a mill, but only if they have a certificate showing they've completed an elementary school course or have a waiver.[46] Under sixteen they are prohibited from working in certain jobs in mills and factories, including adjusting belts, oiling, wiping or cleaning machinery or helping others in these jobs.[47]

There are also laws limiting the working day for children. Under sixteen, the maximum is eight hours a day and six days a week, beginning no earlier than 6 a.m. and ending no later than 7:00 p.m.[48] Children between the ages of sixteen and eighteen are prohibited, except in special circumstances, from working more than nine hours a day or fifty hours a week in mills or manufacturing, but otherwise there are no limits on hours for those over eighteen.[49]

The law provides exceptions. Every law does. In the case of labor laws, there are exceptions for times of emergency or peak demand.[50] There is also authority to suspend the law when "materials and products of which are perishable and require immediate labor thereon to prevent decay thereof or damage thereto" are at stake.[51] This has been interpreted by the Attorney General to apply to the Christmas gift wrapping industry in Vermont. (Waiver for two months may be granted makers of Christmas wrapping tissues of seasonal design of no value after Christmas season.)[52]

The state laws on child labor are administered by the Commissioner of Labor and Industry. This official has broad authority to investigate and recommend enforcement actions through the Attorney General's office of violations of the child labor laws.[53] A copy of the laws on child labor must be posted in every place of business.[54]

If it appears that employment in violation of the child labor laws relating to length of day or week is necessary to "make up time lost on a previous day of the same week, in consequence of the stopping of machinery upon which such child was employed or dependent for employment," then there may be no violation. The law goes on to offer a caveat: "However, stopping of machinery for less than thirty consecutive minutes shall not justify employment at a time not stated in such notice."[55] Legislative history does not explain the reason for this provision.

Each child between the ages of seven and sixteen must attend school a minimum of 175 days a year.[56] The superintendent of the town in which the pupil resides and majority of its school board members may excuse, in writing, a pupil who has reached the age of fifteen years and has completed the work required in the first six years of the elementary school course from further school attendance if his services are needed for the support of those dependent upon him, or for any other sufficient reason.[57]

b. Federal Law. The focus of federal child labor law is "oppressive" child labor. No goods produced within thirty days in which oppressive child labor is employed may be shipped or delivered for shipment in commerce.[58] The exception: if the purchaser acquired the goods in good faith "in reliance on written assurance" that they were not produced with oppressive child labor practices.

Vermont law takes the same sweeping attack on the problem of child labor by prohibiting the sale or possession of any goods produced in violation of the Vermont laws on child labor.[59] In Vermont law, however, there is no good-faith-reliance exception. The fine is a maximum $2,000.

Federal minimum wage and maximum hour restrictions exempt whole categories of employees: outside salesmen, summer camp councilors, those who catch or process fish, small farmers and their families, those who work for small newspapers, babysitters, and computer programmers, among others.[60] Federal child labor laws do not apply to child actors, some child labor during harvest times, newspaper carriers, or those who make wreathes for a living.[61] They do provide explicit directions on what children over sixteen and under eighteen may do working with scrap paper balers and paper box compactors.[62] There are special rules for: the processing of sugar beets and cotton,[63] the employment of those younger than eighteen in the explosives industry[64] and for those engaged in the operation of power-driven woodworking machines.[65]

Sixteen-year-olds cannot drive motor vehicles as employees on public highways. Seventeen-year-olds may drive only during the daytime, if they are licensed, have taken driver's education and wear seatbelts, but are limited to the size and types of vehicles they can drive.[66]

Federal statute does not identify what constitutes "oppressive child labor" practices.[67] Most of the details are left to the Code of Federal Regulations, the enacted rules of the Secretary of Labor. "Oppressive child labor" is defined as employment of a minor in an occupation for which he or she fails to meet minimum age standards of the code.[68] A "minor" is a child under sixteen. As always there are exceptions, for agriculture and certain mining and manufacturing industries, as long as children remain available for education, and for other industries or circumstances.[69] The federal law provides more details and more exceptions than state law.

The Code exempts from its minimum age requirements the employment by a parent of his or her own child, or by a person standing in place of a parent of a child in his custody, except in occupations to which the eighteen-year age minimum applies and in manufacturing and mining occupations. The Secretary of Labor is authorized to require a minimum age of eighteen in certain hazardous jobs.[70]

Unknowing use of child labor is not actionable under federal law, as long as there is a certificate on file showing the child's age. The certificate must be unexpired.[71] Employers are required to insist on a certificate whenever an applicant claims to be one or two years older than the minimum age or claiming to be any age if "his physical appearance indicates that this may not be true."[72] Vermont is among the states that may issue such certificates.[73]

The employment of minors between fourteen and sixteen years of age in the occupations, for the periods, and under specified conditions which do not interfere with their schooling or with their health and well-being, is not be deemed to be oppressive child labor.[74] The general rule is that children fourteen to sixteen may be employed as long as work does not interfere with their schooling or with their health and well-being.[75]

The Code also sets maximum hours for the employment of minors. The rule is a maximum of eighteen hours a week and three hours a day when school is in session and forty hours a week and eight hours a day when school is out.[76] They may not work before 7:00 a.m. or after 7:00 p.m., except during the summer, when 9:00 p.m. is the rule. The exceptions are interesting. Those fourteen and fifteen may work outside those hours as sports attendants and concessionaires.[77]

The question of pre-emption is directly addressed in federal law. State laws governing child labor that establish a higher standard remain unaffected by the federal laws and rules on the subject.[78]

c. Putting the Two Together. By the principles of federalism, federal law pre-empts state and local law when the two are inconsistent and federal law covers that area of law.[79] Where Vermont law provides higher standards, it prevails.

State law prohibiting children under sixteen from beginning work earlier than 6:00 a.m. appears to be pre-empted by a provision of the federal code.[80] Vermont's maximum nine hours a day and fifty hours a week for those sixteen to eighteen is a higher standard than federal law, and so remains good law.[81]

There is no federal minimum age. Vermont's prohibiting employment by those under fourteen in a mill or factory demonstrates a higher standard that remains enforceable.

### 7. Conclusions

Law is strange. If you read it from beginning to end, statutes often seem disjointed and oddly drafted, as if the author was unsure of the outcome. This is a feature of law that has been amended from time to time. Strong laws beget exceptions, variances, and special rules for special circumstances. This is especially true of federal law.

Vermont child labor law shows far fewer signs of meddling by special interest lobbyists. Independent telephone companies do enjoy an exception from the law governing maximum hours for those sixteen to eighteen, for night operators.[82]

The problems with child labor found in the early part of this century have passed now. Occasionally an issue arises, such as the recent controversies involving children in foreign countries making expensive sneakers in "sweat shop" conditions, but for the most part the federal and state laws are self-enforcing and self-correcting if a question arises. Since the adoption of child labor laws in 1867, no child labor case other than those questioning the impact of illegal employment of minors on the applicability of worker's compensation laws has reached the Vermont Supreme Court.[83]

The mills are gone from Winooski now, replaced by shopping malls and housing. The laws that took so long to pass remain in place.

*Paul Gillies is a lawyer/historian. He was born in Burlington and now resides in Berlin, Vermont. He was Deputy Secretary of State (1981-1993) and a member and chairperson of the Berlin Select Board (1993-1998). In 1991, with Gregory Sanford, he edited* The Records of the Vermont Council of Censors. *He writes a regular column on judicial and legal history in the* Vermont Bar Journal.

# Winooski Union Victory in '43 Significant to Vermont
## *by Roberta Strauss*

After a fierce battle by management and the City of Winooski to keep out the union, mill workers elected the Textile Workers Union of America (CIO-TWUA) to be their representative and bargaining agent. The vote, taken June 8, 1943, was 1463 to 1135. It was the third attempt to unionize the American Woolen Company mills at Winooski Falls. On June 9, *The Burlington Daily News* editorialized that the vote was "the greatest victory organized labor has ever won in the state of Vermont."

The American Woolen Company in 1943 was one of the largest producers of woolen and worsted fabrics in the world. World War II production at their Winooski Falls mills included army serge, overcoating, and blankets. Patriotism, democracy, freedom, and justice were central union themes on posters, at rallies and in *Burlington Daily News* ads. "Textiles at War" blared the headline of *The Burlington Daily News* on February 9, with publisher William Loeb's editorial stating, "Textiles are as essential to victory as ammunition, guns, machines, and ships. The Champlain Mills are producing fighting fabrics - looms are guns, weapons of war, banging away hours a day, weaving some of the war fabrics for the armed forces throughout the world. . . . Just as workers

Mill workers at union headquarters, Main Street, Winooski c. 1943. *(Courtesy of Winooski Historical Society)*

aimed their efforts at contributing toward a war victory, the union has aimed its efforts at an election victory."

The unionization effort began behind closed doors. Nine mill employees sent a private letter to the CIO-TWUA in 1941, asking for a union organizer. Soon afterward, the union sent organizer Harold Daoust to visit the Winooski workers. The unionization effort became public on February 6, 1943, when Irwin Jaffe, a national CIO-TWUA representative, spoke to the Lion's Club. The unionization process, set by national law, required that thirty percent of the workers sign union cards, and, after validation by the National Labor Relations Board, a date would be set for a vote by all workers on whether to unionize.

Union organizers focused on issues such as favoritism in the workplace, speedups, equal pay for equal work, seniority and higher wages. After Jaffe's talk, union advertisements began appearing in the *Burlington Daily News* criticizing favoritism in the workplace. Women were perturbed that some male bosses gave better jobs to certain women. The proportion of female workers during the war years was high since many men had been sent off to combat. However, workers' attitudes differed greatly: some were loyal to the company; others felt they had been treated unfairly.

Prominent company men were mill superintendent John

# SWASTIKA OVER WINOOSKI

The Textile Workers Union of America C. I. O. came to Winooski at the request of hundreds of workers of the American Woolen Company. They wanted to join with workers of the 14 other American Woolen Co. mills now under contract with the Textile Workers Union of America C. I. O.

Our campaign has not been secret---We have worked in the open for all to see. Our motives are sound. The workers of Winooski want decent wages, good working conditions, job security and the elimination of favoritism, that has been used to perpetuate the political power of a greedy few---they don't want handouts. The day of paternalism has long since passed.

## THAT WE HAVE JUST BEGUN TO FIGHT
## —DEMOCRACY MUST PREVAIL—
## JOIN THE MOVEMENT NOW

See Your Department Committeeman or Call at Our Office

### TEXTILE WORKERS UNION OF AMERICA CIO
166 COLLEGE STREET, BURLINGTON, VERMONT

From *Chittenden County Historical Society Bulletin* Vol. 27, No. 2 1993.

O'Brien, the mayor, Leo Contois, and an alderman, Maurice Paquette. Paquette was grateful to O'Brien for giving him a job, as his father was unable to work following an accident at the mill.

Other workers told of less pleasant experiences. Interviews unveiled cases of people fired for merely complaining about their jobs. Leola Germaine, a mill worker, stated that the employee's entire family would be fired. Clearly, different experiences led employees to take different stands on the union. Winooski was a small, close-knit mill town (1943 population: 6,036), and relationships of family, friends and neighbors complicated feelings surrounding the union debate.

Winooski government officials were intensely anti-union. Calling Daoust an outsider, Contois, former Mayor John Kelty, Paquette, City Attorney Russell Niquette and others fanned the flames of anti-union opposition. They opened fire in February, denying the use of City Hall for union meetings. Petitions circulated from a Winooski Citizen's Committee bearing the names of eighteen local people, urging mill workers "Don't sign any union card."

Pro-union advocates fired back. John Lawon, a respected union advocate in Barre, called the first statewide union meeting. Meeting delegates charged "We find no democracy in Winooski," and "We know there is no freedom of speech or assembly in Winooski." A bold union advertisement in the *Burlington Daily News* declared "Swastika Over Winooski. . . . The day of paternalism has long since passed. We will not be intimidated. . . the workers of Winooski have our pledge that we are here to stay. We will fight until they are given the opportunity to decide by a secret ballot in a government-supervised election the union of their own choice." A tabloid entitled *Winooski Textile Labor* with the headline "CIO Exposes Phony Front" declared it had unmasked the Winooski Citizen's Committee as a mouthpiece for Winooski politicians, and that the CIO-TWUA had been responsible for all wage increases since 1937 in Winooski.

On June 1, the National Labor Relations Board certified that more than thirty percent of the workers had signed union cards, despite charges by anti-union forces that some signatures were forged or duplicates. An election was set for June 8. Rallies by anti-union forces at City Hall and at the firehouse drummed up opposition, while the union continued to press charges of being denied democratic rights.

The CIO-TWUA victory was big news. The *Burlington Daily News* carried a front-page story. The editorial by Loeb alleged: "If the powers that be had followed American principles and given the union advocates the opportunity of using city hall in Winooski and every chance to state their side of the case, the union would have lost. The moment the union organizers were denied this and that high pressure was brought on this newspaper to stop printing news about the union people began to think maybe they needed a mutual organization such as a union to protect themselves."

Unionization at Winooski mills initiated the spread of unions throughout Vermont. In September 1943, the O.L. Hinds Company of Burlington, a children's clothes manufacturer, Porter Screen Company of Winooski, Central Vermont Public Service Corporation in Rutland and Twin State Gas and Electric Company in St. Johnsbury were unionized. In October, the International Molders and Foundry Workers Union sought elections at the Colley-Wright Company in Waterbury, and ninety percent of the workers at Bullocks Laundry signed union cards. In December, the CIO chalked up victories at Vermont Structural Steel Corporation and the Vermont Spool and Bobbin Company. Bell Aircraft, Burlington's biggest and newest plant, would be next, said organizer Daoust. Union membership rose during World War II nationally. In 1940, twenty-four percent of the workforce belonged to a union; by 1945, the number had risen to thirty-three percent (according to the U.S. Department of Labor, Bureau of Labor Statistics; the Vermont State Labor Council had no information on union membership during World War II).

Statewide union meetings provided the backbone of support for the Spirit of '43 labor movement. After the first meeting in Barre backing the TWUA's Winooski efforts, a second meeting was convened in Winooski. "State labor history was made in Winooski yesterday when Vermont's top-ranking union leaders from all sections met and agreed to establish a harmonious front," reported the media. Roman Catholic clergy lent support as well.

Father William Tennien, from Pittsford, Vermont, came to Burlington in 1941, about the same time as Daoust. Appointed first pastor of St. Mark's Church on North Avenue, Tennien fought for a fair wage scale in the Queen City (Burlington). In a radio sermon on WCAX-Burlington in January 1943, he stated "The low wages in Burlington are nothing more than slavery." Speaking of the wealthy industrialists, Tennien declared, "These modern barons of rape, for they are raping all of humanity; these captains of industry – how high sounding that is – have committed the great crime of the century. They have bled humanity dry." A *Burlington Daily News* headline declared: "Priest Tells of Families Living on $20 Weekly." The average wage in Vermont was 45.1 cents an hour. Rent for a two-bedroom apartment near the mills was $14 per month, excluding heat, light and hot water.

In August 1943, the War Labor Board (WLB) came to Burlington to set a wage scale for the new Bell Aircraft factory. Tennien delivered a speech by Bishop Matthew Brady to the WLB saying "The Catholic clergy is close to these laborers and their families, they know the economic burden due to low wages that oppress them; . . . they know the home conditions and discouragement... The only seeming relief of this condition is strong unionism and the influx of new industries that pay a higher wage."

Some called Bishop Brady's plea to the WLB the "Magna Carta" of labor. Letters of support included one from Democrat Alfred Heininger, unsuccessful candidate for governor of Vermont in 1936 against George Aiken, who wrote: "That was the strongest and noblest support the toilers and the poor of Burlington and vicinity have ever received. How the local 'mighty' must be trembling in their exploiters' seats!"

Tennien, along with Daoust, officiated at the August 9, 1943 ceremony in Winooski giving the CIO-TWUA charter to Local 579. "Don't abuse what you now have because you have a good organization," Tennien said. "All eyes in the state are upon you." Daoust also asked labor to be responsible and to give a good day's work for a good day's pay.

The *Burlington Daily News* reported that most Winooski city officials, citizens, and mill supervisors settled into an atmosphere of harmony after the vote was over. Mill management and the union worked together raising money selling War Savings Bonds and seeking donations to the Vermont War Chest.

The national trend of northern mills closing and moving south where labor was cheaper and not unionized eventually came to Burlington. In 1939, the Burlington Cotton Mill moved south. Some feared that the Winooski mills would do the same, leaving the town shattered. In September 1954, the Textron Corporation bought American Woolen Company. Neither company records nor

*Fortune Magazine* (March 1954), in its story "The Twilight of American Woolen," indicated that the unions had precipitated the sale. According to Textron records, "After World War II, American Woolen did not maintain the same degree of research, styling, and plant modernization effort as some of its competitors, and in consequence of all these factors, there was a decline in sales." As a result, the Winooski mills closed. Strong unionism was not responsible.

Excerpts from Roberta Strauss' article "Unionization Battle in Winooski: Fifty-Year Anniversary" in *Chittenden County Historical Society Bulletin*, Spring 1993, Vol. 27, No. 2., are reprinted with permission of Chittenden County Historical Society.

*Roberta Strauss has a bachelor's degree in psychology and fifth-year certificate from the University of Vermont, and is past president of the Chittenden County Historical Society. She conducted oral history projects (1985-89) on French-Canadian traditions, and labor issues at Winooski textile mills, and produced the video "The Spirit of '43 – The Coming of Age of Labor in Vermont." Her interview tapes and videos are at Special Collections, University of Vermont Libraries.*

### Addendum:

William Loeb may be best known as publisher of the Manchester, New Hampshire *Union Leader*. However, he began his newspaper career in Vermont with the purchase of the *St. Albans Daily Messenger* in 1941, and in 1942, the *Burlington Daily News*. He sided with the TWUA in their struggle with American Woolen Company(AWC) in Winooski, but he paid his own employees low wages. When the printers at the *St. Albans Daily Messenger* tried to organize, he consolidated printing for that newspaper at his non-union Burlington paper. Front-page attention-getting editorials were everyday occurrences for Loeb's newspapers. According to Dr. Robert O'Brien, William Loeb was a good friend of William Muir, resident manager of AWC in Winooski. On one occasion, Loeb asked Muir to send his loom fixers down to the *Burlington Daily News* to repair his printing presses. Despite such help, Loeb wrote scathing articles about AWC management. Dr. O'Brien's father, John O'Brien, was mill superintendent during that time.

# Closure and Renewal

# Why the Mills Closed
*by Douglas Slaybaugh*

The closing of the Champlain Mills in 1954 after more than a century of operation was the most wrenching event in Winooski's history. The Winooski mills were the state's largest employer, with a workforce that peaked at about 3000 during World War II. By 1954 the mills still employed 950 workers. Their layoffs plagued the city with serious unemployment and an over-burdened welfare system for years afterward. Perhaps worst of all, the mills' closing led some to question the city's very reason for being and to suggest that Winooski might have to merge with neighboring Colchester or Burlington.[1]

Why did the mills close? Albert A. Cree, president of Central Vermont Public Service Corporation and a director of the mills' owner, the American Woolen Company (AWC), provided one answer in a meeting held at the Hotel Vermont in Burlington on August 9, 1954 to announce the closing. Cree told the assembled businessmen and community leaders that the Winooski operation "is the most antiquat-

(From *American Woolen Company Mills*, Boston, 1921)

ed and inefficient of any American Woolen Company mill." He added, as a salve to the local community, that "the only reason the Winooski mill[s] continued in operation this far is because of the enthusiasm and action of the people in this area."[2]

Cree's statement that the mills were "antiquated and ineffi-cient," though perhaps accurate, begged the larger question of why they had become so. A fuller explanation of the reasons that would lead to the closing of the Winooski mills had been provided eighteen months earlier in February, 1953 by Francis W. White, AWC board chairman, in the annual stockholders' report. According to White, the company was losing money, more than $6 million in 1952. White attributed the loss to several factors. For one, the demand for woolen fabric had dropped as the public turned increasingly to synthetics which were appealing because of their lower cost and easier care.[3] Another factor was the decline in the defense orders that had been such a boon to the company during World War II and the early years of the Cold War. Perhaps the crucial factor White listed, and one with the most ominous implications for Winooski, was "the continued high cost of labor and manufacturing in our northern mills." White noted the need to wring more concessions from workers in these mills as a way of lowering costs. He announced that AWC would open a third mill in the South by the middle of 1953, and made it clear that if labor concessions were not forthcoming, the company would probably close the Winooski mills.[4] A reason for closing the mills that Cree had only hinted at when he referred to inefficiency, White had made more explicit. From the AWC Chairman's perspective, the blunt fact was that labor costs were too high. Given the loss of government contracts and lower demand for woolens due to the competition from synthetics, workers needed to make wage and benefits concessions or the company would be forced to move even more of its operations into the more business-friendly South.

What made southern mills more competitive than northern mills generally and the Winooski mills specifically? There were a number of factors, some related to climate and some to the business environment. Regarding climate, northern New England frequently suffered from harsh winters while southern winters tended to be mild. This resulted in a large difference in heating costs. Another savings came because it was cheaper to build mills in the South for they did not require special construction to ward off snow and cold. The milder weather of the South also seemed to lower absenteeism.[5]

As with the physical climate, the business climate of the South

Left to right: Mill #1 (burned in 1957), Mills #2 and #3, the Woolen Mill, Winooski, n.d. *(Courtesy of the Woolen Mill)*

also encouraged more efficiency. The federal Tennessee Valley Authority kept power costs in the region low, and southern communities seemed eager to grant generous financial concessions to attract new industry.[6] Finally, labor costs were lower in the South. Historically, the South had been less friendly to unions than the North and wage rates and benefits were significantly lower. In 1954 the Winooski mills paid as much as $1.56 per hour with an added twenty-seven cents per hour in fringe benefits.[7] Raymond Roy, mill superintendent at the time of the closing, believed that the high wages, combined with union pressure to maintain a large workforce rather than accept the introduction of labor-saving machinery, also inflated production costs. Roy charged that the union had once refused to allow the installation of $270,000 worth of new automated machines for the spinning department.[8]

The Chace Mill, Winooski Falls, Burlington, n.d. *(By Louis McAllister, courtesy of Green Mountain Power)*

In the 1953 stockholders' report, Francis White had implied that labor was the prime culprit behind AWC losses. He was more explicit in a January 1954 meeting at company headquarters in New York with Russell Niquette, Winooski city attorney, and Clifton Miskelly, director of the Vermont Development Corporation. Niquette and Miskelly had asked for the meeting in hopes of convincing White to keep the Winooski mills open. White's response was pessimistic, however. As Niquette later told the *New York Times*, "Mr. White made it very clear, without saying it in so many words, that the only way the Winooski mill[s] will be kept running is if the workers agree to increase their work load and take a voluntary pay cut." When Miskelly offered to build a new plant to keep the company in Winooski, White replied that the greatest problem was not the plant itself but the high labor costs. By the end of the month, AWC decided to close eleven New England textile operations, including Winooski's.[9]

Important as high labor costs may have been in the decision to close the mills, Senator George D. Aiken, commenting years later, saw another. Although admitting he did not have proof, he suspected that textile companies like AWC had decided they could come out better financially by closing the mills and gaining tax deductions for business losses than by continuing operations. Whether true or not, the AWC certainly did reject a host of opportunities to keep the mills running longer. Aiken, challenging the claim that declining government business was partly responsible for AWC losses, noted that more defense contracts might have been arranged if the textile companies had been more interested in pursuing them.[10]

AWC also rejected Miskelly's offer to build a new plant. Efforts by some AWC stockholders to hold off closing the mills in New England were brushed aside.[11] Some held out hope that if the Bachman-Uxbridge company bought the mills, they would keep them open, but AWC rejected the other manufacturer's bid.[12] AWC eventually accepted a take-over bid by the cotton and synthetic manufacturer, Textron, which had proposed as early as January 1954, that if it gained control of AWC's New England woolen mills, it would re-evaluate the plan to close them. Textron promised either to keep the mills running or to sell them to companies pledged to keep them running.[13] By the time Textron consummated its take-over in December 1954, however, AWC had shut down the Winooski mills.[14]

For all the efforts to keep them open, it may have been impossible to save the mills for longer than the short run. A threat greater even than southern mills was looming by 1954: foreign competition. Foreign competition was decimating the textile industries of both the United States and Europe by the 1950s and 1960s as former textile importers like Japan and India developed their own industries and began exporting cloth. In Japan's case, the American government encouraged development of such export industries as part of the Cold War effort to build up Japan as an ally and counterweight to communist China.[15] In the late 1930s, before foreign

Mill #4, The Champlain Mill, Winooski. *(By Michael Hill, c. late 1970s)*

competition made inroads and as the nation began to prepare for war, American output of woolen yarn had jumped dramatically. Production peaked in 1944 at 388,000 tons. By 1950, however, production had dipped to 367,000; by 1955 to 317,000. By 1985 production was only 50,000 as AWC production shriveled in the face of cheap foreign imports.[16]

In the long run, it is doubtful that all the labor concessions, tax breaks, and new plant construction imaginable would have been able to save the Winooski mills. The Greater Burlington Industrial Commission (GBIC), which had been organized to hold existing jobs and lure new ones to the area, labored long and hard to keep the mills running, but to no avail. A few years after they closed, however, the GBIC convinced International Business Machines (IBM) to build a plant in Essex Junction. IBM would later become the largest employer in Vermont and a major employer for Winooski residents.[17] Traumatic as the mills' closing was, it did not permanently scar the local community. As Senator Aiken wrote to a Winooski constituent in 1972, "Since the town lost its textile industry it has had better days, better wages, less lay-offs, less relief cases, and a higher population."[18]

AT PUBLIC AUCTION

Thursday, February 14, 1957

AT 10:00 A.M.

**VALUABLE MACHINERY, EQUIPMENT AND SUPPLIES**

OF THE

# CHAMPLAIN MILLS, INC.

On the Premises
WINOOSKI, VERMONT

Sale is by Order of
CHAMPLAIN MILLS, INC.

Under the Management of

## SAMUEL T. FREEMAN & CO.

Established Nov. 12, 1805

— More Than 150 Years Of Selling At Auction —

**Auctioneers**

**80 FEDERAL STREET, BOSTON 10**

1808-10 Chestnut Street, Philadelphia 3

From auction booklet. *(Courtesy of Raymond Roy)*

*Douglas Slaybaugh is department chair and associate professor of history at Saint Michael's College where he has taught U S. history since 1986. An Iowa native, he completed a doctorate in history at Cornell, and has taught at colleges and universities in Texas, New York and Vermont. In 1996, he published the book,* William I. Myers and the Modernization of American Agriculture. *He is currently at work on a dual biography of a married couple, Laurence and Frances MacDaniels, that focuses on their lifetimes of public service from the 1910s to the 1980s.*

# Why I Purchased the Champlain Mill
*by Ray Pecor*

For more than five years, I had an office at Fort Ethan Allen. All those years, from 1971 to 1976, I drove past the Champlain Mill. Each time I would say to myself, "What a great building, what a great location, someone should do something with this beautiful building." In fact, my grandparents had worked at the Mill. We wanted to put the Champlain Mill on the Historic Sites list and have this wonderful building get the credit it deserved. Let's try to make it something special! Let's try to make it stand out in our community! Let's try to have the city and its residents proud of this great building!

There was a great deal of discussion about downtown Winooski during those times. Model City Grants were in the works and Winooski was going through an uplifting phase for their downtown. But what about the focal point, the Mill? What to do and who would do it? A complete change could not happen to downtown Winooski until this building returned to what was in 1912, a great-looking building. That was my vision.

Bernard Healy, a developer from Massachusetts, had bought the Mill and the land to the east and to the northwest. He built a supermarket and drug store to the east and a bank to the northwest but did not want to tackle the Mill itself. So, after saying for years, "Someone should do something with this wonderful building, and no one is stepping up to do it," I said, "Let's talk to the city and see how they would feel about me getting involved."

Peter Clavelle, the city manager at that time, was very encouraging. I then met with Bernard Healy. He wanted to sell. The city owned the land where the parking lot is, so I had to negotiate with them for that parcel. In September 1978, I made a deposit with Healy; the dream of making this beautiful building active again was on its way. The City of Winooski loaned me $700,000 for thirty years at eight percent. This money came from a Model Cities grant from the federal government.

The Mill had been closed for years; the building had sustained a lot of damage during the time it was vacant. Windows were blown out; bricks were discolored and damaged; the roof leaked; and the interior was in shambles. Interior columns, ceilings and walls needed sandblasting to remove discoloration caused by rain and

The Champlain Mill, derelict c.1978. *(Courtesy of the Champlain Mill)*

pigeons coming in through the roof and broken windows. The sandblasting also polished the rough columns to give them a comfortable feel and to avoid splinters. There was so much oil in some parts, we couldn't get it out. We chemically cleaned the exterior to preserve the bricks, and replaced the broken windows with glass having the same green tint as the original ones.

A new roof, the only major change, was necessary to protect the building. The clerestory on top had wooden framing that needed to be removed because it would not withstand the load of the new roofing material. The landscaping was designed not to distract from the building's features.

The shopping, office and restaurant ideas came from many meetings with business colleagues Dudley Davis, P.C. Kirby, Pat Robins and architect Jim Lamphere from Burlington, and Boston architect Mare Rector who

The Champlain Mill, restored c.1982. *(Courtesy of the Champlain Mill)*

was involved in Boston's Faneuil Hall project. Implementation followed what the city would allow us to do.

The Champlain Mill reopened in September of 1981 with a grand ceremony that I could not attend. I was in bed with three herniated disks in my back. My wife and Dick Snelling, former governor of Vermont, were there. Jack Barry, a local radio announcer, substituted as master of ceremony.

*Ray Pecor, owner of the Lake Champlain Transportation Company in Burlington, Vermont, has developed shopping centers and industrial parks. A successful businessman, he has also contributed to the Burlington area through investment in renewal such as the office building on the site of Burlington's Strong Hardware which burned, as well as Winooski's Champlain Mill. The Heritage Winooski Mill Museum owes its existence to his generous donation of hall and gallery space in the Champlain Mill.*

# The Champlain Mill: Adapting Architectural Features
## *by James Lamphere*

The E.W. Pittman Company of Lawrence, Massachusetts built the Champlain Mill in 1909. The major products of the Mill were piece-dyed worsteds; smooth surfaced yarn for weaving, knitting, and serges; and silky fabrics for suits and dresses. The Mill was a major economic force in Winooski.

The existing four-story mill was constructed of heavy timber and brick with a full basement and a wood-framed penthouse (clerestory). Located adjacent to the Winooski River, this building features arched window and door openings around the exterior. As a focal point of the structure, there is a stair and elevator tower on the west side of the building. The interior is open with exposed brick walls and heavy timber framing that were in good condition; the flooring was in extremely rough condition.

Prior to Ray Pecor's purchase of the property in 1978, we walked through the vacant structure to review with Ray his ideas of how the building should be used. His intentions were to make it a mixed-use facility, with the first three floors dedicated to commercial use and the top two levels and penthouse to be developed as residential space. During this walk-through, we noted a few main features:

1) The river, if exposed to the users of the building, would be a strong aesthetic feature, yet its location on the south side with the main entrance on the north side, made it difficult to take advantage of.

The Champlain Mill on the Winooski River. The top story is a clerestory, a windowed wall construction used for light and ventilation. *(From* American Woolen Company Mills, *Boston, 1921)*

2) The large wide-open spaces and the large windows provided some key elements for the uses that Ray wanted to bring into the building.

Our original design scheme provided for an entrance at center on the north side with a lobby that cut through the building, leading to a monumental staircase that opened up a view to the river and connected all levels of the commercial space. Unfortunately, this scheme needed a large area for circulation, making it impractical from a financial point of view from the non-rental to rental space ratio.

(Courtesy of Special Collections, University of Vermont Libraries)

With our original idea not feasible, we had to take a step back and look further at the layout of the structure. By this time in our research process we had met with numerous developers, city boards, and the architect who developed the waterfront in Baltimore and Faneuil Hall in Boston. We learned that we should have a goal of leasing forty percent of the commercial space for restaurant use. This had been a key factor in the success of similar projects. Since the Mill, constructed of heavy timber, was a combustible structure, the state building code would not allow restaurants or assembly spaces above the first floor or level of discharge, because it would be harder for patrons to vacate the facility in the event of a fire.

In the final design, the bridge entrance was conceived to provide a "level of discharge" above the lowest level. This would provide grade-level access at three levels, and would allow for restaurant and assembly use on all levels of commercial space. We also discovered that the design for residential use was not efficient, and that the clerestory structure had over-stressed the existing columns and had to be removed. After obtaining approval from the Division for Historic Preservation, this was accomplished.

A Floor of the Champlain Mill after the mills shut down. *(By Michael Hill)*

As noted earlier, one of the major features of the building was the large arched windows. Such large expanses of glass created a problem from an energy standpoint. Another energy concern was that the exterior walls were of solid uninsulated brick construction. Our first choice was to leave the perimeter walls exposed rather than to insulate and cover them with sheet rock. We were able to retain the exposed brick walls and keep the large arched window openings with new insulated glass by incorporating a water-source heat pump system to heat the building. This efficient system, in this application, transfers solar heat gain from the large southern exposure to other parts of the building. Our mechanical design team was able to show that, by using a water-source heat pump system, we could retain the building's interior brick surface, be efficient from a heating standpoint, and meet the energy code of 1988. In the final analysis, we were able to retain the major features of this historic structure, make the building efficient from an operating standpoint, and put one of the major structures in the city of Winooski back to a practical use.

*James Lamphere is a retired senior partner of Wiemann-Lamphere Architects in Colchester, Vermont. He and his firm were involved in planning and redesigning the derelict Champlain Mill of the 1970s into an attractive landmark at Winooski's city center.*

# The History of Winooski One
## by John Warshow

The development of waterpower at the falls in Winooski commenced with the arrival of settlers of European ancestry. Throughout New England during the eighteenth and nineteenth centuries, growing numbers of settlers sought locations to efficiently harness the power of falling water to turn wheels to grind grain, saw lumber, and manufacture basic necessities.

In Winooski, Ira Allen built the first waterpowered mills in 1783 for the manufacture of iron and lumber and the grinding of grain into flour. The mills were located on both sides of the upper falls. From these humble beginnings arose the City of Winooski, home of the most substantial mill complex in Vermont, employing thousands of people. The mill development reached its peak between 1875 and 1950, beginning in 1901 under the auspices of the American Woolen Company.

Subsequent changes in technology, labor, textiles, the environment, and the availability of energy resources resulted in the mills closing during the mid-1950s. For the first time in nearly two hundred years, the great water wheels of Winooski were idle.

Following turbulence in world energy markets in the 1970s, and with increasing recognition of environmental problems associated with burning fossil fuels and nuclear power, state and national energy policies changed. These changes resulted in the construction of a new modern hydroelectric station, park, and fishway at the lower falls in 1992, continuing a centuries-long tradition of harnessing the power of falling water in Winooski, Vermont.

There is little record of the specific technology utilized in the late 1700s and early 1800s to harness the waterpower in Winooski. Water wheels constructed of wood were common in New England at the time. They were either "overshot," meaning water was supplied to the top of the wheel and its weight spun the wheel until the water spilled out at the bottom, or "undershot," where the water pressure pushed the wheel causing it to spin. The water wheel was coupled to a shaft. This slow-spinning shaft, connected to gearing to increase speed, turned belts and more shafts, transferring power to turn grinding stones to produce flour or vegetable seed oil, to move a saw for lumber, or to run simple machinery for manufacturing.

As manufacturing grew in scope and complexity, so did the development of waterpower in Winooski. Cast iron water wheels or "turbines" were first used in the late 1800s. These turbines needed less maintenance, were highly efficient, and spun at higher speeds, all of which allowed for more power development and, therefore, more manufacturing. In the late 1800s, construction of a new and larger dam at the lower falls, expanded canals and waterways, numerous powerhouses, more and larger mill buildings, and the development and use of electricity (generated by water-driven turbines) culminated in a massive industrial mill complex at Winooski Falls. The power-

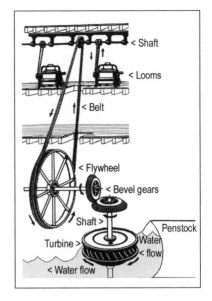

The mechanical transfer of waterpower to looms. *(Redrawn from* Handbook 140, *U.S. Department of the Interior)*

houses, penstocks, flumes, intakes, and canals were notable parts of this impressive development, which provided the energy to power and light the mills and power an electric trolley which ran to Burlington.

After nearly forty years of abandonment, from 1956 to 1993, the waterpower has once again been harnessed. Three turbines with a combined capacity of 10,000 units of horsepower provide 7,400 kilowatts of electric power at the Winooski One Hydroelectric Station. The hydroelectric station converts the power of falling water into electric energy. As water flows from the intake at the upstream side of the powerhouse through the turbines, it forces the propellers of the turbines to spin. The water then flows out the backside of the powerhouse into the tailrace downstream.

The spinning propellers, or "runners," transmit the mechanical power to the electric generators via shafts and gears. Inside the generator, the rotor, which is attached to the spinning shaft, spins at 720 r.p.m. inside a fixed assembly called a stator. The rotor is a large electromagnet; the stator is composed of tightly wound copper wires. The rotor spinning inside the stator creates an electric current in the stator. High voltage wires transmit the current to the electric distribution system. In the control room, switchgear and computers control the turbine and generators. Recognizing that floods have periodically damaged the mills and powerhouses at Winooski Falls, the new station, built of reinforced concrete, is designed to be watertight and completely submerged during a major flood event.

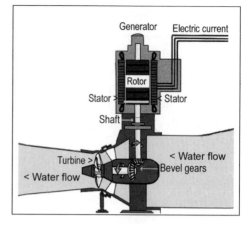

The mechanical transfer of waterpower to electric current. *(Courtesy of Winooski One Partnership)*

The power is purchased by the State of Vermont through a purchasing agent for each electric utility in the state and all of their customers. It provides just under 1% of all the electricity consumed in Vermont.

*John Warshow is a partner of Winooski One Partnership, based in Montpelier, Vermont. In 1992, the Partnership built a hydroelectric station at the lower falls, the site in earlier years of waterpowered woolen mills and a gristmill. The Partnership operates several other small hydroelectric stations in Vermont.*

# Epilogue
## *By Dana Lim vanderHeyden and Jeffrey Good*

The fabric of Winooski is woven of many threads: ethnic, economic and spiritual. As the essays and oral histories in this book show, the story of this speck on the map of Vermont - barely one mile square - tells itself in voices that represent a remarkable variety of humankind.

In the last two centuries, Winooski residents have come from vastly different backgrounds: Irish immigrants escaping the worst famine in their country's history, Armenians fleeing a nightmare of political violence, French Canadians thirsting for work. They joined Poles, Italians, Syrians, Lebanese and Abenakis to build a place that is not just a city, but a community.

Many came for the promise of work at the textile mills, red-brick beacons of opportunity rising from the banks of the Onion River. Every night, the workers and their families would drift to sleep to what Edward Boyajian called a "serenade," the clackety-clack of the looms from across the river. The community that grew up around the mills offered plenty of sweetness: enlightening lectures for the mill workers in the evenings, cherry tarts at the Star Bakery, and hymns to God welling up from Saint Francis Xavier and other houses of worship. There was pride, too. As John O'Brien recalled, the city could boast that most G.I.s in World Wars I and II had slept beneath blankets made by the American Woolen Company.

But there were also harsh words and hard times. In the 1940s, mill workers pushed for the right to unionize, with vocal backing from members of the Catholic clergy. Their efforts, opposed by mill managers and the local political leaders, succeeded. But a decade later, the mills closed, with high labor costs cited as one factor. The shutdown plunged Winooski into a depression from which it has taken decades to recover.

At many of those difficult times - the floods of the 1920s, the Great Depression of the 1930s, the mill closings and more recent debates over school quality - Winooski might have appeared to outsiders as a place whose future was bleak. Yet Winooski residents held together. By focusing on their families, their religious faith and their sense that this was a place worth fighting for, they did more than survive. They thrived.

From our perch here in Winooski Park, we at Saint Michael's College take a particular pride in Winooski and our connection to it. Many sons and daughters of the city trudged up the hill for their education and then returned to make Winooski a better place. World War II veterans from the Class of 1950 have fond memories of escaping to the American Restaurant. And, as the stories in this book attest, Saint Michael's professors and graduates have more than a passing interest in Winooski's past - and future.

On June 5, 2000, as this publication was being completed, Winooski native son Raymond Roy, who had dedicated a good part of his life to the American Woolen Company mills, died in his home on Union Street. A part of Winooski disappeared with Mr. Roy, along with his radiant smile, twinkling eyes and gentlemanly demeanor. Nevertheless, he had always shared his recollections and stories of the "old days," inspiring many of us to learn about and from the past. Through him and others like him – particularly the authors of these essays – the legacy of Winooski will be passed on to coming generations as they build a new future for their beloved Winooski.

*Dana Lim vanderHeyden, a member of the Advisory Board of Héritage Winooski since its inception, has pursued an academic career for nearly 30 years — first as an assistant professor of French and, more recently, as a college administrator — in Pennsylvania and New York. Currently, she serves on several non-profit boards in Vermont, including Alliance Française/Cercle Québécois, Vermont Public Radio and Burlington City Arts. Her husband, Marc, is the fifteenth president of Saint Michael's College.*

*Jeffrey Good, a journalist and author, recently launched the Centennial History Project at Saint Michael's College to mark the college's 100th birthday in 2004. Good, a 1981 graduate of Saint Michael's, won the Pulitzer Prize in editorial writing and is co-author of the book,* Poison Mind. *He and his wife, Laura Dintino, had their first apartment on Spring Street in Winooski. They now live in Montpelier with their children, Amelia and Alexander.*

### "The Abenaki and the Winooski" by Frederick M. Wiseman

1. Salmon Hole is across from the Woolen Mill, just below the falls.
2. The Iroquois "faded" as well. Not one Mohawk village survived in New York.
3. Kevin Dann, "From Degeneration to Regeneration: The Eugenics Survey of Vermont, 1925-1936," *Vermont History*, Vol. 22, no. 1 (Winter 1991), 5-29.
4. Genocide or ethnic cleansing is the deliberate destruction of a culture either by prohibition of its practice or ensuring that the practitioners disappear by sterilization or murder.

### "Damn the Dams: The Impact of Dams on Streams" by Daniel Bean

1. For explanations and examples of various levels for these parameters see dauntless.smcvt.edu, a web site maintained by the National Science Foundation Rivers Program at Saint Michael's College, or Mark K. Mitchell and William B. Stapp, *Field Manual for Water Quality Monitoring*, 11th ed., (Dubuque, Iowa: Kendall/Hunt Publishing. Co., 1997), an environmental education program for schools, or any basic limnology (fresh water) textbook.
2. In 1920, Vermont was 80% deforested; today it is about 80% forested.
3. Old growth forest, the final stage in the succession of growth from the earliest stage, usually grass or shrub growth to the typical "natural forest" of an area.
4. Mill #1, a large six-story building, was producing textiles by 1837; it burned in 1957.

### "French Canadian Émigrés and Industrialization" by Betsy Beattie

1. According to the marriage records for St. Joseph's parish as compiled by Véronique Gassette, all but one of the couples whose Quebec marriages were recorded in St. Joseph parish records had been married in the Montreal District of Lower Canada. Of these, over one-half had been married in parishes of the Richelieu Valley. See Véronique Gassette, *Mariages de St. Joseph de Burlington, Vermont, 1834-1930* (Montreal: Éditions Bergeron et Fils, 1978), xxv-xxx.
2. Robert Rumilly, *Histoire des Franco-Américains* (Montreal: L'Union Saint-Jean-Baptiste d'Amérique, 1958), 29-30.
3. See the chapter by Ouellet, "The Establishment of Parliamentary Institutions," in Paul G. Cornell, Jean Hamelin, Fernand Ouellet, Marcel Trudel, *Canada: Unity in Diversity* (Toronto: Holt, Rinehart and Winston of Canada, 1967), 158-160.
4. Susan Mann Trofimenkoff, *The Dream of Nation: a Social and Intellectual History of Quebec* (Toronto: Gage Publishing Ltd., 1983), 72.
5. Mason Wade, "French and French Canadians in the U.S.," in *A Franco-American Overview*, ed. Madeleine Giguère, 4 vols. (Cambridge, Mass.: National Assessment and Dissemination Center for Bilingual/Bicultural Education, 1981), 3:38.
6. The administration of Governor James Craig was a particularly oppressive one for the French Canadians. Craig imposed a new land tax on the peasantry during a period of crop failures and depression; he planned to use the money to build a prison. Among those he chose to imprison were the editors

of *Le Canadien*, a French newspaper which opposed the policies of his administration. For a discussion of Craig's actions, see Ouellet, "Birth of French Nationalism," in *Canada: Unity in Diversity*. For a reference to emigration of French Canadians during Craig's administration, see Wade, "French and French Canadians in the U.S.," 38.

7. Yolande Lavoie, *L'Émigration des Québécois aux États-Unis de 1840 à 1930* (Québec: Éditeur Officiel, 1979), 4.

8. Ralph Dominic Vicero, "Immigration of French Canadians to New England, 1840-1900: a Geographical Analysis" (Ph.D. diss., University of Wisconsin, 1968), 111-112.

9. Wade, "French and French Canadians in the U.S.," 39.

10. Lavoie, *L'Émigration des Québécois aux États-Unis*, 7-9.

11. Vicero, "Immigration of French Canadians to New England," 90.

12. Rumilly, *Histoire des Franco-Americains*, 29.

13. Georges Langlois, *Histoire de la Population Canadienne-Française* (Montreal: Éditions Albert Levesque, 1934), 173.

14. Peter Haebler, "Habitants in Holyoke; the Development of the French Canadian Community in a Massachusetts City, 1865-1910" (Ph.D. diss., University of New Hampshire, 1976), 26.

15. Iris Saunders Podea, "Quebec to 'Little Canada': the Coming of the French Canadians to New England in the Nineteenth Century," in *The Aliens: a History of Ethnic Minorities in America*, ed. Leonard Dinnerstein and Frederic Cople Jaher (New York: Appleton-Century-Crofts, 1970), 208

16. Vicero, "Immigration of French Canadians to New England," 97-99.

17. Trofimenkoff, *The Dream of Nation*, 135.

18. Ibid.

19. Canada, Legislative Assembly, *Report of the Select Committee of the Legislative Assembly, Appointed to Inquire into the Causes and Importance of the Emigration from Lower Canada to the United States* (Montreal: Rolls Campbell, 1849), (1).

20. Ibid., passim.

21. Ibid., passim.

22. Canada, Legislative Assembly, "Report of the Special Committee on Emigration", *Appendix to the Journals of the Legislative Assembly of the Province of Canada* 15 (1857), passim.

23. Trofimenkoff, *The Dream of Nation*, 133.

24. William MacDonald, "The French Canadians in New England," in A Franco-American Overview, ed. Madeleine Giguère, 4 vols. (Cambridge, Mass: National Assessment and Dissemination Center for Bilingual/Bicultural Education, 1981) 10.

25. See pages 15-23 in "Émigrés and Industrialization: French Canadians in Burlington and Colchester, Vermont, 1850-1870" for an explanation of the *Patriote* movement and the Rebellions.

26. Mason Wade, "The French Parish and Survivance in Nineteenth Century New England," in *A Franco-American Overview*, ed. Madeleine Giguère, 4 vols. (Cambridge, Mass.: National Assessment and Dissemination Center for Bilingual/Bicultural Education, 1981), 3:235.

27. Joseph Amrhein, "Burlington, Vermont: The Economic History of a Northern New England City" (Ph.D. diss., New York University School of Business Administration, 1958), 70.

28. Amrhein, "Burlington, Vermont," 241.

29. One reason the Burlington Woolen Mill found the transition to a peacetime economy so easy was that by 1865 police forces in most cities were organized into municipal departments and wore uniforms. According to James F. Richardson in his history of police protection in America, "as the number of the unskilled and propertyless rose with immigration and farm-to-city movement, people who believed in the values of efficiency and authority succeeded in imposing uniforms upon policemen, servants and railroad conductors. New York's police became uniformed in 1853, Philadelphia's in 1860 and Chicago's in 1861." See James F. Richardson, *Urban Police in the United States* (Port Wshington, N.Y.: Kennikat Press, 1974), 28; W.S. Rann, *History of Chittenden County, Vermont* (Syracuse, N.Y.: D. Mason and Co., 1886), 464.

30. Rann, *History of Chittenden County*, 464.

31. Wade, "French and French Canadians in the U.S.," 40.

32. Lavoie, *L'Émigration des Québécois aux États-Unis de 1840 à 1930, 25.*

33. Robert Rumilly, *Histoire des Franco-Américains*, 40.

34. Alexandre Belisle, *Histoire de la Presse Franco-Américaine* (Worchester, Mass.: Ateliers Typographique de *L'Opinion Publique*, 1911), 63-64.

35. Wade, "French and French Canadians in the U.S.," 40-41.

36. Iris Saunders Podea, "Quebec to 'Little Canada," 207.

37. T.D. Seymour Bassett, "Urban Penetration of Rural Vermont, 1840-80" (Ph.D. diss., Harvard University, 1952), 580.

38. Amrhein, "Burlington, Vermont," 74-75.

**"In the Shadow of the Factory: Worker Housing in Winooski" by Susan Ouellette**

1. Although to refer to factory workers as "operatives" might evoke a negative stereotype in our own time, nineteenth century workers and management alike held a different view. Newspaper articles, industrial reports and factory workers themselves routinely referred to "operatives" and meant to imply a positive and active participation in the industrial revolution that was changing their world before their eyes.

2. For more specific information on Lowell and the Waltham System see Thomas Dublin, *Women at Work: The Transformation of Work and Community in Lowell, Massachusetts, 1826-1860.*

3. David J. Blow and James N. Hunt Sr. *Look Around Winooski, Vermont*, ed. Lilian B.Carlisle (Burlington: Chittenden County Historical Society, 1972), 6.

4. Payment of cash wages after deduction of living expenses was standard for the time. A contemporary newspaper article on the Winooski mill pointed out that "a large number of operatives ... have been uniformly and promptly paid in cash for their services." See "The Burlington Mill Company," *Burlington Free Press*, 23 May 1849, 2:1.

5. Blow and Hunt, *Look Around Winooski, Vermont*, 7.

6. United States Census, 1850 Manuscript Population Schedules, Vermont, Chittenden County, Town of Colchester, Winooski Village.

7. This is based on a sample of five boarding house populations from the 1850, 1860, 1870, 1880, 1900 and 1910 census.

8. Blow and Hunt, *Look Around Winooski, Vermont*, 7.

9. One 1850 editorial lauds the range of entertainment available in the Burlington/Winooski area and suggests that even more emphasis should be made to provide evening entertainment in the winter months. *Burlington*

*Daily Free Press*, 19 January 1850, 2:1

10. For more information about working women's resistance see Mary Blewett, *We Will Rise in Our Might: Working Women's Voices From Nineteenth Century New England.*

11. "Strike Among the Spinners," *Burlington Daily Free Press*, 6 February 1865, 2:1

12. "The Burlington Mill Company," *Burlington Daily Free Press*, 4 June 1849, 2:3.

13. United States Census, 1850, 1860, 1870, 1880, 1900, 1910, Manuscript Population Schedules, Vermont, Chittenden County, Town of Colchester, Winooski Post Office.

14. *Vermont: A Guide to the Green Mountain State*, Federal Writers' Project, (Boston: Riverside Press, 1937), 51.

15. Blow and Hunt, *Look Around Winooski, Vermont,* 21.

16. Blow and Hunt, *Look Around Winooski, Vermont,* iii.

## "Mill Photographers" by Jeffrey Marshall

1. Lewis W. Steponaitis Jr., "The Textile Industry of Vermont, 1790-1973: Its Development, Diffusion and Decline." (Master's thesis, University of Vermont, 1975), 66.

2. Naomi Rosenblum, *A World History of Photograph.* (New York: Abbeville Press, 1984), 131-43.

3. David J. Blow and James N. Hunt Sr., *Look Around Winooski, Vermont*, ed. Lilian B.Carlisle (Burlington: Chittenden County Historical Society, 1972), 2-6.

4. Kim Borsavage, *L. L. McAllister: Photo-Artist.* (Burlington: Robert Hull Fleming Museum, 1979).

5. Naomi Rosenblum, *World History of Photography*, 325-32. McAllister's photographic archives, including hundreds of panoramas are in Special Collections, University of Vermont Libraries.

6. Beaumont Newhall, "Lewis Wickes Hine," in *Dictionary of American Biography, Supplement Two*, 305.

7. Walter Rosenblum, "Foreword," in Lewis Hine, *America & Lewis Hine: Photographs, 1904-1940.* (New York: Aperture Inc., 1977).

8. Vermont, *An Act Concerning the Education of Children between Eight and Fourteen Years of Age*, Public Acts, no. 35, 1867.

9. Vermont, *An Act Relating to Public Instruction*, Public Acts, no. 20, 1892; Vermont, *An Act in Amendment of Section Six of Number Twenty, Laws of 1892, Entitled "An Act Relating to Public Instruction,"* Public Acts, no. 18, 1894.

10. Freddy Langer, "Lewis W. Hine: Man and Work," Introduction to Lewis W. Hine, in *The Empire State Building.* (Munich: Prestel, 1998), 19-21.

11. "James Detore: A Photographic Memory." *Vermont Quarterly.* (August 1989), 16-22. Detore's archive of photographic negatives is in Special Collections, University of Vermont Libraries.

## "Regulating Child Labor in Vermont" by Paul Gillies

1. Leon S. Gay, "Woolen Manufacturing in Vermont," *Vermonter* 47 (September 1942), 118-21, 128.

2. The 1777 Vermont Constitution provided that "no male person born in this country, or brought from over sea, ought to be holden by law, to serve any

person, as a servant, slave, or apprentice, after he arrives to an age of twenty-one years; nor female, in like manner, after she arrives at the age of eighteen years, unless they are bound by their own consent, after they arrive to such age, or bound by law for the payment of debts, damages, fines, costs, or the like." In 1924, an amendment to Article 1 revised the law to provide independence when both men and women became twenty-one.

3. Lorenzo D'Agostino, *The History of Public Welfare in Vermont* (1948), 180.
4. 1837, Ch. 24.
5. House Journal (1867), 255.
6. *Id.* at 355-356.
7. "An Act in relation to the hours of labor of children employed in manufacturing and mechanical establishments," No. 36 (1867)
8. "An Act concerning the education of children between eight and fourteen years of age." No. 35 (1867).
9. See Lawrence Friedman, *A History of American Law* (2nd ed., 1985), 561; D'agostino, *supra*, 181.
10. No. 9 (1888), §§ 154-156, 158.
11. No. 26 (1894).
12. Winston Allen Flint, *The Progressive Movement in Vermont* (1941), 75.
13. "An act relating to the employment of child labor." No. 155 (1904).
14. No. 52 (1906).
15. No. 69 (1910).
16. No. 70 (1910). In 1915, a law was enacted requiring employers to "provide chairs, stools or other contrivances for the comfortable use of . . . female employees [working as clerks], for the preservation of their health and for rest when not actively employed in the discharge of their respective duties," regardless of age. No. 209 (1915).
17. Flint, *supra*, 75-76.
18. *Id.* at 79, citing a report in the BFP on December 12, 1912.
19. No. 75 (1912), § 10.
20. Id., § 5.
21. No. 85 (1919).
22. Minutes of the House Committee on Commerce and Labor, March 10, 1937 (H. 255), Vermont State Archives, Redstone.
23. No. 176 (1937).
24. No. 130 (1943).
25. No. 4, (1987); No. 144 (1987) (Adj. Sess.).
26. Hammer v. Dagenhart, 247 U.S. 251 (1918). David E. Kyvig, Explicit and Authentic Acts: Amending the U.S. Constitution, 1776-1995 (1996), 255.
27. Holden v. Hardy, 169 U.S. 366 (1898).
28. Muller v. Oregon, 208 U.S. 412 (1908).
29. Champion v. Ames, 188 U. S. 321 (1911).
30. Hipolite Egg Co. v. United States, 220 U. S. 45 (1911); Hoke v. United States, 227 U.S. 308 (1913).
31. 247 U.S. at 272.
32. Id.
33. 247 U.S. at 280.
34. Kyvig, supra, 256.
35. Bailey v. Drexel Furniture Co., 259 U.S. 20, 37-38 (1922).
36. See Kermit L. Hall, William M. Wieck, Paul Finkelman, American Legal History: Cases and Materials (1991), 399.

37. BFP 2/17/1925.

38. See Minutes of House Committee, supra.

39. Unlike other constitutional amendments proposed by Congress, the child labor amendment did not have a seven-year deadline. Technically, it could still be adopted.

40. See George Aiken, Speaking From Vermont (1938); D. Gregory Sanford, "You Can't Get There From Here: The Presidential Boomlet for Gov. George D. Aiken, 1937-1939," 49 Vermont History 197-208 (1981).

41. It was a different story with Workmen's Compensation. Vermont watched as the New York courts declared that state's efforts unconstitutional in 1911. Flint, supra, 84-85. Before passing such laws, the Vermont Constitution was amended in 1913 to give the General Assembly direct authority to "pass laws compelling compensation for injuries received by employees in the course of their employment resulting in death or bodily hurt, for the benefit of such employees, their widows or next of kin." Vt. Const. c. 1, sec. 70.

42. Schechter Poultry Corp. v. United States, 295 U.S. 495 (1935).

43. U. S. v. Darby, 312 U.S. 100 (1941).

44. 312 U.S. at 115-116.

45. 21 V.S.A. § 436. The prohibition includes working in canneries, workshops, or any manufacturing business.

46. 21 V.S.A. §§ 431, 433.

47. 21 V.S.A. § 437.

48. 21 V.S.A. § 434.

49 21 V.S.A. § 440.

50. 21 V.S.A. § 441.

51. 21 V.S.A. § 452.

52. 1938-40 Op. Atty. Gen. 262.

53. 21 V.S.A. §§ 446, 447.

54. 21 V.S.A. § 442.

55. 21 V.S.A. § 443.

56. 16 V.S.A. §§ 1071, 1121.

57. 16 V.S.A. § 1123(c).

58. 29 U.S.C.A. § 212(a).

59. 21 V.S.A. § 453.

60. 29 U.S.C.A. § 231(a).

61. 21 U.S.C.A. § 213(c)(1), (2), (3), & (4); (d).

62. 29 U.S.C.A. § 213(c)(5

63. 29 U.S.A. § 213(i), (j).

64. 29 C.F.R. § 570.51.

65. 29 C.F.R. § 570.55.

66. 29 U.S.C.A. § 213(c)(6).

67. 29 U.S.C.A. § 212(c).

68. 29 C.F.R. § 570.1(b).

69. 29 C.F. R. § 570.2(a)(1)(i).

70. 29 C.F.R. § 570.2(a)(1)(ii).

71. 29 C.F.R. § 570.5.

72. 29 C.F.R. § 570.5(c).

73. 29 C.F.R. § 570.9.

74. 29 C.F.R. § 570.31.

75. 29 C.F.R. § 570.31.

76. 29 C.F.R. § 570.35(a).

77. 29 C.F.R. § 570.35(b).

78. 29 C.F.R. § 570.50.

79. Duffy v. Brannen, 148 Vt. 75, 83 (1987).

80. 21 V.S.A. § 434.

81. 21 V.S.A. § 440.

82. Id.

83. See *Wlock v. Fort Dummer Mills*,98 Vt. 449 (1925); *Brace v. Bashaw*, 114 Vt. 366 (1947); *Grenier v. Alta Crest Farms, Inc.*, 115 Vt. 324 (1948); *Bruley v. Fonda Group, Inc.*, 157 Vt. 1 (1991).

## "Closure and Renewal" by Douglas Slaybaugh

1. "Champlain Mills to Close," *Burlington Free Press* (*BFP*), August 10, 1954, 1; "Textile Future of Winooski Hinges on Community, Says Cree," *BFP*, August 10, 1954, 1; "Real Challenge to Industrial Ingenuity," editorial, *BFP*, August 11, 1954, 6; "GBIC Votes to Build Plant to Keep Textile Industry Alive in Burlington Area," *BFP*, August 11, 1954, 9; Lynn Cline, "Champlain Mill History: The Mills Were No Worse than Working on the Farms," *Vermont Cynic*, October 8, 1981, 41, Winooski-Champlain Mill folder, University of Vermont (UVM) Special Collections; *A Report to the Citizens of Winooski, Vermont for the Year Ending December 31, 1953*, (Burlington, Vermont: Queen City Printers, n.d.), 1, 8, 22, 23; *A Report to the Citizens of Winooski, Vermont for the Year Ending December 31, 1954*, (Burlington, Vermont: Queen City Printers, n.d.), 4, 5, 11, 25; *A Report to the Citizens of Winooski, Vermont for the Year Ending December 31, 1955*, (Burlington, Vermont: Queen City Printers, n.d.), 8, 22, 26; *A Report to the Citizens of Winooski, Vermont for the Year Ending December 31, 1956*, (no pub., no place, n.d.), 11, 26.

2. "Champlain Mills to Be Shut Down by September 30," BFP, August 10, 1954, 1.

3. "American Woolen Expands in South," New York Times, February 12, 1953, 35. For testaments to the popularity of synthetics at the time the Winooski mills' fate was being sealed, see M. G. Ramey, "Man-made Fibers Change the Picture," Country Gentleman, March, 1954, 123-28+; "Man-made Fibers Are Coming into Their Own," House Beautiful, June, 1954, 96-97; and N. Carlisle, "New Wonder Fabrics for Your Clothes," Coronet, February, 1955, 78-82.

4. "American Woolen Expands in South."

5. Cline, 41; Raymond Roy interview transcript, Roberta Strauss interviewer, November 24, 1986, Special Collections, University of Vermont Libraries, 48-50.

6. "Textile Future of Winooski Hinges on Community;" "Real Challenge to Industrial Ingenuity;" Roy, 49.

7. "Bid Made to Keep Wool Mill Open," New York Times, January 8, 1954, 30.

8. Roy, 46-48.

9. "Bid Made to Keep Wool Mill Open;" "Century Old Mill to Close," New York Times, August 10, 1954, 28.

10. Aiken to James N. Hunt, Sr., June 6, 1972, "Winooski, Vt." Folder #2, Special Collections, University of Vermont Libraries. That Aiken may have been optimistic about the willingness of the government to save northern mills is suggested in "American Woolen Elects 4 to Board," *New York*

*Times*, January 28, 1954, 37. The article reports the refusal of the Eisenhower administration to intervene to stop the closing of two AWC mills in Lawrence, Massachusetts, despite the request of Congressman Thomas J. Lane.

11. "Wool Plan Opposed," New York Times, January 19, 1954, 38; "Woolen Holders Propose a Delay," New York Times, February 2, 1954, 31.

12. "Whither Now," editorial, Burlington Daily News, June 11, 1954, n.p., "Winooski-Champlain Mill" folder, Special Collections, University of Vermont Libraries.

13. "American Woolen Gets Textron Bid," New York Times, January 29, 1954, 29.

14. New York Times, December 17, 1954, 47.

15. James Foreman-Peck, A History of the World Economy: International Economic Relations since 1850, (Totowa, N.J.: Barnes & Noble Books, 1983), 279-81, 294, 307; "22 Nations to Fight Drop in Textile Pay," New York Times, February 14, 24; Thomas J. McCormick, America's Half-Century: United States Foreign Policy in the Cold War, (Baltimore: Johns Hopkins University Press, 1989), 88-89.

16. B. R. Mitchell, International Historical Statistics: The Americas, 1750-1988, (New York: Stockton Press, 1993, 2nd ed.), 375-76.

17. "Textile Future of Winooski Hinges on Community;" "GBIC Votes to Build Plant to Keep Textile Industry Alive in Burlington Area," BFP, August 11, 1954, 9; Paul Heffernan, "IBM Joins Queue in Equity Market," New York Times, May 19, 1957, III, 12.

18. Aiken to Hunt.

## REFERENCES

**"The Fuller's Teasel" by Peter Hope**

Buchanan, Rita. *A Weaver's Garden.* Loveland, Colorado: Interweave Press, 1987, 180-182, 186-189.

Gleason, Henry A. and Arthur Cronquist. *Manual of Vascular Plants of Northeastern United States and Adjacent Canada*, 2nd ed. Bronx, New York: New York Botanical Garden, 1991.

**"Transportation Conditions Affecting Winooski Wolen Manufacturing" by T.D. Seymour Bassett**

Amrhein, Joseph. "Burlington, Vermont: The Economic History of a Northern New England City." Ph.D. diss., New York University, 1958, xi, 351, 6 leaves.

Steponaitis, Lewis W., Jr. "The Textile Industry of Vermont, 1790-1973: Its Development, Diffusion and Decline." Master's thesis, University of Vermont, 1975.

Wilgus, William J. *The Role of Transportation in the Development of Vermont.* Montpelier, Vt.: Vermont Historical Society, 1945. See maps by Earle Williams Newton and the author.

**"The Methodist Episcopal Church and the Mill Community" by Linda M. Howe**

Blow, David J. and James N. Hunt Sr. *Look Around Winooski, Vermont.* Edited by Lilian B.Carlisle. Burlington: Chittenden County Historical Society, 1972.

Harding, C.L. and W.C. Harding. *Quit-Claims Deed to the Stewards of the 2nd M.E. Church*. Vol. #16, 315, 434, Winooski City Hall archives.

Epworth League of the Methodist Episcopal Church. *1899 Winooski Vt*. Burlington: P.C. Dodge, 1899.

**"First Come, First Served": Proverbial Wisdom from the World of the Millers and the Mills" by Wolfgang Mieder**

Dent, Robert W. *Shakespeare's Proverbial Language: An Index*. Berkeley, California:Univiversity of California Press, 1981.

Hulme, F. Edward. *Proverb Lore*. London: Elliot Stock, 1902; rpt. Detroit, Michigan: Gale Research Company, 1968.

Mieder, Wolfgang. *American Proverbs: A Study of Texts and Contexts*. Bern: Peter Lang, 1989.

Mieder, Wolfgang. *Proverbs Are Never Out of Season: Popular Wisdom in the Modern Age*. New York: Oxford University Press, 1993.

Mieder, Wolfgang, Stewart A. Kingsbury and Kelsie B. Harder (eds.). *A Dictionary of American Proverbs*. New York: Oxford University Press, 1992.

Simpson, John A. *The Concise Oxford Dictionary of Proverbs*. 2nd ed. Oxford: Oxford University Press, 1992.

Stevenson, Burton. *The Macmillan (Home) Book of Proverbs, Maxims and Familar Phrases*. New York: Macmillan, 1948.

Taylor, Archer. *The Proverb*. Cambridge, Massachusetts: Harvard University Press, 1931; rpt. ed. by Wolfgang Mieder. Bern: Peter Lang, 1985.

Taylor, Archer, and Bartlett Jere Whiting. *A Dictionary of American Proverbs and Proverbial Phrases, 1820-1880*. Cambridge, Massachusetts: Harvard Universiy Press, 1958.

Tilley, Morris Palmer. *A Dictionary of the Proverbs in England in the Sixteenth and Seventeenth Centuries*. Ann Arbor, Michigan: University of Michigan Press, 1950.

Titelman, Gregory. *Popular Proverbs & Sayings*. New York: Random House, 1996.

Urdang, Laurence, Walter W. Hunsinger, and Nancy LaRoche (eds.). *Picturesque Expressions: A Thematic Dictionary*. Detroit, Michigan: Gale Research Company, 1985.

Whiting, Bartlett Jere. *Chaucer's Use of Proverbs*. Cambridge, Massachusetts: Harvard University Press, 1934; rpt. New York: AMS Press, 1973.

Whiting, Bartlett Jere. *Proverbs, Sentences, and Proverbial Phrases From English Writings Mainly Before 1500*. Cambridge, Massachusetts: Harvard University Press, 1968.

Whiting, Bartlett Jere. *Early American Proverbs and Proverbial Phrases*. Cambridge, Massachusetts: Harvard University Press, 1977.

Whiting, Bartlett Jere. *Modern Proverbs and Proverbial Sayings*. Cambridge, Massachusetts: Harvard University Press, 1989.

Wilkinson, P.R. *Thesaurus of Traditional English Metaphors*. London: Routledge, 1992.

Wilson, F.P. *The Oxford Dictionary of English Proverbs*. 3rd ed. Oxford: Oxford University Press, 1970.

**"Winooski Union Victory in '43 Significant to Vermont" by Roberta Strauss**

*Burlington Daily News*, 1943: January 22, p. 1; February 6, passim.; March 17, p. 1; April 5, passim.; May 5; June 1, passim.; June 9; August 9, passim.;

August 19, p. 1, 9; September 18, passim. October 8, pp.1; 11, 28; November 4, pp.3, 13; December 22, pp.1; 24.

*Brattleboro Reformer*, 4 September 1934, 1.

Cash, Kevin. *Who the Hell is William Loeb?* Manchester, N.H: Amoskeag Press, Inc., 1975.

*City of Winooski 22nd Annual Report 1935-1944.* Winooski City Hall.

Davitian, Lauren-Glen, "The Frogs Across the Pond: Perceptions of Change in a Vermont Mill Community." Nuquist Paper, Center for Research on Vermont, University of Vermont, 1983.

Judd, Richard Munson. *The New Deal in Vermont: Its Impact and Aftermath* New York: Garland, 1979, 130, 153-159.

Minutes of Winooski City Council Meeting, Vol. 4. 1941-45; January-June, 1943. Winooski City Hall.

Oral Histories, Special Collections, University of Vermont Libraries and Center for Research on Vermont: William & Dolly Kirby; Esther Mintzer; Maurice Paquette; Leola Germaine; Father Edward Gelineau.

Saunders, Dero A. "The Twilight of American Woolen." *Fortune Magazine.* (March 1954), 95, 198.

*Textile Labor.* (2 July 1949), 6.

*Textron Inc.*, Providence, Rhode Island, 7 Feb 1955.

*Vermont Legislature Directory and State Manual*, 1989-90, Fletcher Free Library, Burlington, Vermont.

# Contributors

T.D. Seymour Bassett, author and retired archivist, University of Vermont.

Daniel Bean, professor emeritus of biology, Saint Michael's College.

Betsy Beattie, Canadian Studies librarian, University of Maine.

David J. Blow, author and retired archivist, University of Vermont.

Lucy, Edward and Steve Boyajian, daughter and sons of an Armenian immigrant mill family.

Kim Chase, second-generation bilingual Franco-American, French teacher and author.

Laura Deforge, native and long-term resident of Winooski.

Vincent Feeney, realtor; author and adjunct professor of history, University of Vermont.

Connie Stech Flynn, former mill worker and daughter of a Polish immigrant mill family.

Paul Gillies, lawyer; historian; former deputy secretary of state for Vermont.

Jeffrey Good, journalist and author, Montpelier.

Clarke Gravel, lawyer; former state's attorney and judge of probate, Burlington.

Larry Handy, Winooski native and son of a Lebanese immigrant family.

Peter Hope, biology instructor, Saint Michael's College.

Linda M. Howe, educator, University of Vermont; Winooski resident.

James Lamphere, retired senior partner, Wiemann-Lamphere Architects, Colchester.

Jeffrey D. Marshall, archivist and curator of manuscripts, Unversity of Vermont.

Wolfgang Mieder, professor of German and folklore, University of Vermont.

Nicholas Morwood, lawyer and son of a Syrian immigrant mill family.

Gail A. Nicholas, active in politics and third-generation member of a Syrian immigrant family.

John O'Brien (1892-1984), former general manager of American Woolen Company mills, Winooski.

Robert E. O'Brien, physician; advisory board, Héritage Winooski; Saint Michael's College trustee; Winooski native.

Susan Ouellette, assistant professor of history, Saint Michael's College.

Ray Pecor, owner, Champlain Mill, Winooski; entrepreneur and benefactor.

Frank Perrino, Winooski native; former baker and mill worker; son of an Italian immigrant mill family.

Madeline Perrino, long-time Winooski resident; former mill worker; daughter of an Italian immigrant family.

Raymond Roy (1916-2000), former superintendent, American Woolen Company mills; Winooski native.

Douglas Slaybaugh, associate professor of history, Saint Michael's College.

Roberta Strauss, oral historian; author; former president, Chittenden County Historical Society.

Jennie G. Versteeg, former professor of economics, Saint Michael's College; business consultant, Ottawa, Canada.

Bert Villemaire, coordinator of assessment and instruction, Winooski Middle/High School; Winooski native.

Dana Lim vanderHeyden, advisory board, Héritage Winooski; college associate, Saint Michael's College.

John Warshow, advisory board, Héritage Winooski; partner, Winooski One Partnership.

Frederick M. Wiseman, member of the Abenaki Nation; professor of humanities, Johnson State College.